Your Business Is a Success
Now What?

The Wiley Small Business Series

For the small business owner, success or failure often depends on the day-to-day management of hundreds of business problems and details. Drawing on the knowledge and experience of experts, these concise, detailed handbooks offer you sound advice and vital practical help on every aspect of managing a small business—sales, financing, accounting, advertising, security, and taxes—everything you need to operate a successful business. Look for them in your favorite bookstore.

Titles in the Series

Your Business Is a Success
Now What?

Gregory F. Kishel
Patricia Gunter Kishel

A Wiley Press Book
JOHN WILEY & SONS, INC.
New York • Chichester • Brisbane • Toronto • Singapore

Publisher: Judy V. Wilson
Editor: Alicia Conklin
Managing Editor: Maria Colligan
Composition & Make Up: Ganis and Harris, Inc.

Library of Congress Cataloging in Publication Data
Kishel, Gregory F.,
      Your business is a success: Now what?

      (Wiley small business series)
      Includes index.
      1. Small business.   2. Success.   I. Kishel,
Patricia Gunter. II. Title. III. Series.
HD62.7.K583 1983   658'.022   82-24745
ISBN 0-471-87699-2

Printed in the United States of America

84 85 10 9 8 7 6 5 4 3 2 1

This book is dedicated to
Joseph and Josephine Kishel
Henry and Pauline Smith

Acknowledgments

We would like to acknowledge the following people for their support and encouragement in the writing of this book: Alicia Conklin, Michael and Eileen Ferris, Forrest and Linda Harding, Dianne Littwin, Cheryl McDonald, Kathleen Mulcahy, Joseph Perry, Randall Stuart, and Jon and Judy Tavel.

Contents

Introduction

As management consultants, we have written this book for the person who is already a successful entrepreneur or would like to be. Picking up where other business books leave off, at the point when business decisions are more complex and the stakes are higher, it focuses on the new challenges facing every successful business owner:

- How large should my business grow?
- Should I branch out into other areas?
- How much control do I really need?
- What's the best way to boost employee morale?
- What about time for my family?

Exploring these questions and more, *Your Business Is a Success: Now What?* will assist you to evaluate the various options from which to choose. Designed to help you maximize your success, it has these unique features:

Going beyond the basics of starting a business, each chapter addresses a *key decision area* of concern to business owners (planning, expansion, personal involvement, control, and so on). Whatever your current situation, you will find the advice and information you need to make the right choices.

Successful entrepreneurs across the United States share their strategies for building and maintaining a profitable business. Representing large and small businesses in fields ranging from high fashion to high technology, services to manufacturing, each entrepreneur takes you behind the scenes of his or her business.

Business profiles located at the back of the book provide you with additional information on the entrepreneurs and enterprises and serve as a convenient reference. Rather than saving these for last, we urge you to turn to them as often as you like. This will enhance your enjoyment of our book.

1 The Turning Point

Where Do You Go from Here?

MOMENTUM is the primary concern during the initial stages of starting a business—getting the business going and keeping it going. Each day of operation, each new customer served, each dollar received represents a victory, bringing your business closer to that dream of success. But as all successful business owners ultimately discover, success isn't so much a destination as a turning point. Having reached it, there are new challenges to face.

The question that invariably arises is, "Now what?" Should you expand your business or keep it at its present size? Franchise? Add or drop products? Raise or lower quality standards? Change the image? Become more involved or less involved in the day-to-day operating decisions? The seemingly endless list of choices can be both intriguing and intimidating. Yet how you cope with them is crucial to the future success of your business.

Maintaining Your Success

"The wolf is away from the door," says Peter Van den Beemt. "But the pressure now is really the same pressure it's always been. How do we cope with what's going on around us? From day to day the circumstances change."

The success of his business, Wordplay, a do-it-yourself word processing center that provides users with access to computerized printing and information storage, is a case in point. In establishing the center, Peter adds that he and his two partners "learned how to cope with yesterday, but we're still learning how to cope with today."

Though obviously enjoying her success in the beauty industry, Marie Vega confesses to feeling "like a boat in the middle of the ocean. I could spring a leak at any time." Known as "the haircutter to the Hollywood Stars," in addition to having her own salon and cutting the hair of such celebrities as Peter Lawford and Erik Estrada, Marie manufactures a line of hair and skin products through her own company, Marie Vega & Associates. An astute business woman as well as an accomplished hair stylist, she says, "I don't think there is any climbing up to a certain place and staying there. Not anymore. In the old days you could build a company and it would become established and go on and on and on. . . . Now, the next day you could make one mistake and go down the drain."

Lina Lidow estimates that Lina Lee, the high-fashion, North Rodeo Drive boutique she started in 1977, reached the turning point midway between its third and fourth year. Recalling that time, she says with a laugh, "I always thought that once I reached the top I could, all of a sudden, sit back and start taking care of myself. Instead of working seven days a week, I'd cut it down to four, maybe three. I could really start relaxing and be the elegant shop owner, walking in in my three-piece suits and my high heels, instead of my bermudas, cotton shirts, and flat shoes that I wear because I run so much. . . . But nothing changed."

Lina finds that if anything, she's working harder than ever. "The hardest thing," she says, "is realizing that once you reach the top, staying there is another thing. Now that I know we're successful and we do have that loyal clientele, every season they expect me to discover the newest person, always to have the most unusual thing. So when they go to a party, they aren't there with their fifteen closest friends, all dressed in the same thing that's available at twenty different stores. That constant pressure is still on me not to disappoint the customers."

Not only is the pressure still on once your business reaches the turning point, but, as Annie Hurlbut found out, the stakes are higher, too. Co-owner of The Peruvian Connection, a mail-order company specializing in sweaters, blankets, ponchos, and other luxury items in alpaca, she says, "Things like 'losses' suddenly become *big* mistakes." What's more, given the higher stakes involved, "personal worth is no longer adequate as a bailout option."

According to Doug McDonald, of Planning Counselors, Incorporated, the turning point isn't so much a time to ease back on your business as to reevaluate it. Referring to his own company, which sets up and administers corporate pension plans, he says, "It got to the point where business began to come to us, rather than us going to it. That was a real transition, to go from being out there hustling, trying very hard to get clients, to the point where our reputation had preceded us." In dealing with this situation, PCI made the decision to drop some of its customers so that it could offer better service to the ones it kept. As Doug explains it, "the biggest thing is reallocating your resources from pushing so hard to achieve the business to realizing that *doing* the business competently is what's going to maintain the place you've already achieved."

Although letting your customers go is never easy, especially in light of the effort that went into getting them in the first place, sometimes it's necessary. In PCI's case, the company discovered that certain clients were actually *costing* it money. Whether it was because they paid late, tied up staff members with an inordinate amount of questions, created too much paperwork, or whatever, they were not generating a profit for the company. To turn this situation around, the only alternatives were to charge more or let them go. Rather than raise its prices, PCI decided on the latter move. In effect, it agreed to accept a reduction in its gross revenue. However, the payoff came later. By reducing its costs and reallocating its resources to give better service to its other accounts, the net profit actually improved.

Thus the turning point is more than a time to savor your success. It's a time to reevaluate your current needs and plan for the future.

The Business Life Cycle

To understand better what the turning point is and how it can affect the development of your business, it helps if you look at it in the context of your business' entire life cycle. From beginning to end, the business life cycle looks something like this:

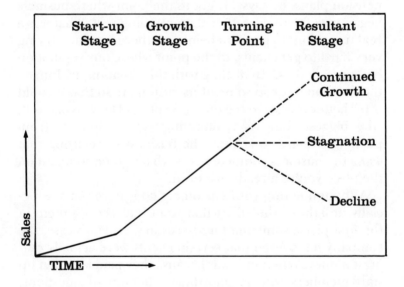

As you can see, the life cycle of a business has four distinct stages: start-up, growth, turning point, and resultant. Each stage plays a critical role in your business' development and in shaping what your business is or becomes. Unless progress is halted somewhere along the way—because of internal forces (the owner's actions) or external forces (the environment)—all businesses go through each of these stages.

The start-up stage is that period when the idea of starting a business is converted into reality. It encompasses such preliminary activities as researching the market, preparing a business plan, and obtaining financing, along with the actual mechanics of opening your doors and commencing operations. This includes selecting the legal structure for your business, setting up the books, choosing a location, staffing, controlling inventory, promoting, and insuring the business.

The growth stage happens when the business becomes established in its field and begins to expand its customer base. It's a time characterized by change as your business develops its own identity and carves out a niche in the marketplace. At the peak of this stage your business should recover all or most of its start-up costs and make a profit.

The turning point occurs when the business has achieved its initial goals and is now positioning for the future. Both new opportunities and new obstacles arise as your business confronts the challenges ahead. Decisions made during this stage virtually have the power to make or break the venture.

The resultant stage is that period when the business becomes fully developed. What happens in this stage is a direct result of the decisions made at the turning point. At this time your business can go in a number of directions, with growth subsequently increasing, leveling off, or decreasing. The longer this stage lasts, the more likely it is that other turning points will occur. These, in turn, may further alter the course of your business.

How you handle the turning point in your business will determine, to a major extent, what happens in the resultant stage. Unfortunately, many business owners pass through the turning point without even realizing it, because they are either too busy to notice it or don't recognize it when they see it. When that happens, problems often occur. Several things can go wrong, such as the following: quality starts to drop; production gets out of sync, jumping ahead of or falling behind the number of orders; costs increase; employee morale sags; customer relations suffer. What causes these things to happen? They happen because the business continues to follow the original plan it started with, rather than modifying it or replacing it with a plan better suited to new circumstances.

Take the area of customer credit: A strategy that made sense in the beginning may no longer be appropriate. Offering credit to your customers may have helped to build up your sales volume, but as a result of that practice, finance costs have begun to cut severely into your profits. Unless something is done about this, you could be in trouble. Having recognized the problem, the question is, "How do you resolve it?" Should you raise prices? Offer a discount to cash customers? Eliminate the use of credit cards altogether? Whatever you decide to do, there is the risk of losing potential customers. The need to come up with a workable solution to a problem like this is typical of the challenges that must be faced at the turning point.

Annie Hurlbut describes The Peruvian Connection's turning point as an "awkward teenage" phase. During this time, she found "things were still too small to benefit from economy of scale, yet staggeringly big when manual operations were involved." Given that, the major question facing Annie was whether to expand, or more specifically, how deep a commitment to make. The question has been partially answered, but it is yet to be totally resolved.

Sue Jones-Allen faced a similar situation. The owner of

Up Against the Wall, an interior contracting firm that does everything from creating original murals and wall coverings to remodeling, she made the mistake of expanding too quickly. Having done so, she says, problems with quality control caused her to rethink the matter. In addition to this, she wasn't really happy with the new work arrangements. In Sue's words, "After trying an office situation—files, desks, manager, etc.—this drove me wild!" She soon decided to move her business back to its original location—her home, or to be precise, her van.

Now that the business is in her home again, Sue says, "I am always in my van and on the go. No one ever needs to come to me. I go to them. [In dealing with the turning point] the obvious answer was to keep it all in the van. Life improved 100 percent. I always have what I need at hand. It's much more workable."

The Importance of Planning

Reaching the turning point is no small feat. Overcoming start-up obstacles and building your business into a venture capable of competing in the marketplace take skill and dedication. Entrepreneurs who succeed tend to be savvy risk-takers, good problem-solvers, and alert spotters of new opportunities. In many instances, though, they have had little experience with planning. Often their business ideas were converted into realities through action rather than through long-range planning. Now, however, given the greater number and magnitude of the decisions to be made, the need for an overall business plan takes on a new importance.

Research shows that lack of planning can undo a growing business. To succeed over the long haul, a plan must be devised to take into consideration each area of operation—production, marketing, finance, administration control, and so on. Without such a plan to direct and coordinate the various activities of your business, it's easy to get into a situation where your right hand doesn't know what your left hand is doing.

Doug McDonald of Planning Counselors, Incorporated is well aware of how important it is to have a business plan and also how easy it is to avoid preparing one. "Sometimes it's difficult to find the time to do two- and three-year forecasts when I also have some client's work that I need to get out," says Doug. Part of the problem is the fact that a plan is not something that's immediately productive. Unlike manufacturing a product or making a sale, a plan's value won't be known until later. As Doug sees it, "in the long run, 'nonprofit' activities like planning and training are what are going to make you successful."

Because of the nature of Doug's business—setting up and managing corporate pension plans—the majority of his clients are themselves successful businesspersons. But, ironically, according to Doug, not all of them are good planners. Explaining the reason for this, Doug says, "People who become successful immediately are the worst planners because they feel that they don't need to plan. . . . They start making widgets and they keep making them. Getting successful means that they make more of them. The attitude is, 'What we've done in the past worked, so why not do the same thing bigger and better now?' " But in so doing, they forget to look at the changes that have occurred; and they forget to reevaluate their customers' needs, the competition, and the economy.

Your Business Plan

To prepare your business plan or modify an existing one, the *first step* is to *define* the nature of your business and its *ultimate objectives*. For instance, you might state that yours is a catering business and its ultimate objectives are to (1) be known for its quality and originality, (2) have a reputation for dependable service, (3) be sought after for the best parties, (4) gross $250,000 per year from catering, and (5) manufacture and distribute a line of frozen gourmet foods.

The *second step* is to communicate your objectives to those employees and others (your banker, accountant, and so on) whose help you need to realize your objectives. In this way, rather than working in the dark or at cross purposes, everyone can join forces for maximum results. This also enables you to get feedback, which might have a bearing on your plan of action, and helps to create a sense of belonging among employees.

The *third step* is to forecast or predict the future, based on the data available (financial records, newspapers, magazines, government reports, surveys, your own observations, and so on). Your purpose in this is to discover new trends that might affect the demand for your product or service. In the case of the catering business, you might discover that with more women working, the demand for frozen gourmet foods is going up, because working women have more money to spend and less time to cook.

The *fourth step* is to inventory your resources for achieving your objectives. This means taking stock of your assets—those that show up on a balance sheet and those that don't. Do you have the money, inventory, equipment, and facilities that it will take to achieve your objectives? In addition, do you have the technical knowledge, staff, and level of personal commitment to carry out all the tasks associated with your objectives? If not, will you be able to obtain the resources you need?

The *fifth step* is to set intermediate goals and a timetable for achieving your objectives. This means outlining the sequence of events that must take place to reach your destination. To continue our example, if the catering business decides to enter the frozen-foods market, it must do the following: (1) develop recipes; (2) create a brand name and image; (3) set up, or contract with, a food-processing facility to produce the product; (4) arrange for distribution; and (5) plan an advertising campaign. Given the need to coordinate these activities and to make efficient use of your resources, deadlines should be set for completing each task.

By taking the time to formulate your objectives in this way and to map out a strategy for achieving them, you will be in a better position to capitalize on any opportunities that arise. Better yet, rather than always being forced to react to change, you will be better equipped to anticipate the change before it occurs. This gives you the edge in determining how to make the most efficient use of your resources. Instead of cranking out more widgets when the demand for them is dropping, you can reduce your output until the demand goes back up. You may even decide to create a "new and improved" widget that has greater appeal, or even to go into a totally different market.

Success on Your Own Terms

In setting the objectives for your business, it's absolutely essential to set your own personal objectives as well. What do you as an individual want? Will achieving the goals of your business enable you to achieve your personal goals, too?

Probably as much has been written about the high price of success as the joys of attaining it. Just what *is* the price of success? Are you willing to pay it?

When Up Against the Wall reached the turning point, Sue Jones-Allen notes that one of the major challenges was "not allowing the tail to wag the dog. It was at this point that I became quite enamored with my success and nearly alienated my family." Compounding the problem was an illness that sidelined Sue for two months. Recovered and wiser from the experience, she says, "It proves that you can't push beyond the limits forever. I had to learn to protect myself [from the constant demands of the business]. Now I take much better care of myself."

The price of success can be strained personal relationships; physical and mental breakdowns; disenchantment; boredom; loss of creativity; and the feeling that you're missing out on something, are unappreciated, or worse. Yet it doesn't have to be any of these. The closer your personal objectives are to those of your business, the lower the price of success. This comes from having a business that enables you to satisfy your needs, rather than demanding that you sacrifice them.

To find out if your personal objectives and those of your business coincide, take a few minutes to answer the two questionnaires that follow. The first one, "Indicators of Personal Success," should help you to clarify what's necessary for your personal success. The second, "Owner's Activities Necessary for Business Success," should help you to clarify what's necessary for the success of your business.

INDICATORS OF PERSONAL SUCCESS

Success Indicators	Very Important	Moderately Important	Relatively Unimportant
1. Financial security	———	———	———
2. The opportunity to be creative	———	———	———
3. Time to myself	———	———	———
4. Time with my family	———	———	———
5. Good health	———	———	———

Continued on page 24

Indicators of Personal Success, Cont'd

Success Indicators	Very Important	Moderately Important	Relatively Unimportant
6. Control over my environment	_____	_____	_____
7. Recognition from my family	_____	_____	_____
8. Recognition from my peers	_____	_____	_____
9. Recognition from the public	_____	_____	_____
10. Low degree of stress	_____	_____	_____
11. A well-run home	_____	_____	_____
12. A flexible schedule	_____	_____	_____
13. An affluent lifestyle	_____	_____	_____
14. An active social life	_____	_____	_____
15. Good friends	_____	_____	_____
16. Challenging work	_____	_____	_____
17. Being a good parent	_____	_____	_____
18. Involvement in civic and political activities	_____	_____	_____
19. Being able to travel	_____	_____	_____
20. A good education	_____	_____	_____
21. Maintaining an attractive personal appearance	_____	_____	_____

OWNER'S ACTIVITIES NECESSARY FOR BUSINESS SUCCESS

Necessary Activities	Very Important	Moderately Important	Relatively Unimportant
1. Working long hours	_____	_____	_____
2. Business travel	_____	_____	_____
3. Investing in the business	_____	_____	_____
4. Meeting deadlines	_____	_____	_____
5. Producing the product or providing the service	_____	_____	_____
6. Selling the product or service	_____	_____	_____
7. Coming up with new ideas	_____	_____	_____
8. Business planning	_____	_____	_____
9. Working nights	_____	_____	_____
10. Working weekends	_____	_____	_____
11. Day-to-day management	_____	_____	_____
12. Taking risks	_____	_____	_____
13. Moving to another city	_____	_____	_____
14. Public speaking/ promotion	_____	_____	_____
15. Attending meetings	_____	_____	_____
16. Doing paperwork	_____	_____	_____

Continued on page 26

Owner's Activities Necessary for Business Success, Cont'd

Necessary Activities	Very Important	Moderately Important	Relatively Unimportant
17. Talking on the telephone	_____	_____	_____
18. Handling person-nel or union problems	_____	_____	_____
19. Obtaining capital	_____	_____	_____
20. Dealing with investors	_____	_____	_____

What indicators of personal success did you check as being very important to you? Financial security? Time to spend with your family? An active social life? These should be compared with those activities you must perform to have a successful business: traveling, obtaining capital, taking risks, and so on. By comparing your answers on the two questionnaires, you can determine whether your personal objectives are being fulfilled through your business, fulfilled in spite of your business, or perhaps not fulfilled at all. If the first instance is true, you are one of the lucky ones who has found a way to have success on your own terms. However, if the second or third instance is the case, the price of success has escalated. In this event, you have the option of paying it, or you may wish to redefine your definition of success. Should you decide to do this, the turning point of your business may become a personal turning point as well.

2 Big, Bigger . . . Best?

One Size Doesn't Fit All

ONCE your business is successfully established, growth becomes a key issue. How large should it grow? Does "bigger" equate with "better"? Each business owner must decide what size best suits his or her business and plan accordingly. Just as some entrepreneurs favor an aggressive expansion program, others make a conscious effort to keep their business small.

Barbara Koch describes her gift shop, Outstanding Stuff, as "Five hundred square feet, jam-packed, ceiling, floor, walls, shelves, everything. It's completely full." Handpainted ceramic masks, velvet dragons, whimsical folk toys, and decorative boxes are just a few of the unusual or one-of-a-kind gifts Barbara carries. "There are things in my shop that you won't find even on the streets of New York," she says proudly. "To put my shop together, you would have to go to probably thirty different shops. . . . And here it is in one little corner, all together."

Barbara attributes much of her shop's success to its small size. "The most important thing I did in selecting my location was to find a feasible size so that the rent wouldn't kill me. I have seen store after store after store go down the tubes because it was too big, the rent was too high. . . . No matter what you sold, it was never enough. If I had to, I could go to the bank and scrape up the rent money, if I couldn't meet it for whatever reason. But if my rent were three thousand dollars a month, I would have a real tough time." Consequently, Barbara advises, "Anybody in business should keep it as simple and clean as possible."

Her own advice notwithstanding, Barbara is still open to the possibility of future growth: "I would like to expand and have other branches. But," she says, "there's a serious problem in finding responsible employees. I've had partners. I've had employees. And, time and time again, they've disappointed me. People want it all and they want it easy. It's hard to find someone who wants to work from the ground up." So until she can find someone willing to work as hard as she does, Barbara is keeping Outstanding Stuff a size that's "manageable by me."

When Richard LaMotta invented the Chipwich, three and a half ounces of premium ice cream sandwiched between two chocolate chip cookies with the exposed ice cream rolled in chocolate chips, he had no idea that his creation would become so popular. At least not so soon. On May 1, 1981, he started selling the Chipwich from sixty vending carts throughout New York City. Less than two hours later, all eighteen thousand Chipwich sandwiches were sold out. Richard recalls, "We didn't have any more. I said, 'What do we do now?' Things were flying so fast and furious, it was selling out so quick that my immediate problem turned to one of financing growth. We needed a second factory."

Thus, Richard's decision to grow so large so fast wasn't made by him alone but by the growing demand for the Chipwich. Chipwich, Inc., the multimillion-dollar company Richard literally started in his father's basement in Brooklyn, now has its headquarters in Manhattan and factories located throughout the United States. Since its debut on the streets of New York, the Chipwich has spread across the country. In addition to being available from the familiar sidewalk carts, it can be purchased at 7-Eleven stores, Haagen Dazs ice-cream shops, grocery stores, department stores, hotels, and other outlets, not to mention onboard coast-to-coast airline flights.

"When I went into it I wasn't thinking this will make me a millionaire. It gave me independence and creativity. I thought I'd get a little New York business going," says Richard. Now he has had to set new goals for himself, such as eventually having ten thousand carts in the United States and worldwide distribution of his product.

Developing an Expansion Policy

In selecting a course of action—to expand or not to expand—you'll want to consider such factors as cost, efficiency, quality, service, control, and personal satisfaction. Will increasing the size of your business have a positive or a negative effect on these areas? The advantage of lower unit costs must be weighed against the disadvantage of higher overhead; the potential for enlarging your market share against the risk of reducing quality and service, and so on.

Cost

At first glance, the costs associated with expanding your business may appear obvious. These include remodeling costs, if your present site is to be expanded; rent or mortgage payments, if a new location is added; equipment, furniture, and fixtures costs; and increased payroll and insurance expenses. But there are other costs, too, the costs of *not* expanding your business. These include lost sales because of an inability to keep up with customer demand; higher unit costs because of inefficient production methods; higher employee turnover costs because of lack of opportunities for advancement.

In other words, it can cost you whether you expand or

not. To determine whether further growth will enable your business to be more cost-effective, the costs of expanding must be compared with those of not expanding.

For Herb Reiner, expanding helped his business become more competitive. Herb owns Vitamin City, a chain of discount vitamin stores. For one thing, he saves money on purchases: "We're starting to buy some of our faster-moving items direct from the manufacturers. That's where the savings come in, in the bulk rate. So there is an advantage to having more than one store. The average health food store cannot really compete with us."

Thus, a larger business may be able to achieve "economies of scale" that a smaller business cannot achieve. These economies stem from the ability to buy, produce, and sell products in large quantities, thereby lowering individual unit costs. All the same, the smaller business has an advantage of its own, which shouldn't be forgotten: lower overhead.

Efficiency

Will expanding your business make it more efficient or less efficient? This depends on the nature of your product or service and your objectives. If your goal is to sell shoes to as many people as possible, then increasing the number of stores and salesclerks available to serve potential customers could improve your efficiency level.

The thing to beware of, however, is expansion of an existing location, or addition of a new one, without adequate assessment of the demand for your product. Unless demand is sufficient to justify the new expansion, it could end up reducing your overall efficiency and draining profits from the rest of your operation.

Herb Reiner says that with vitamins, "You're not dealing with the average person on the street. You're dealing with 8 to 10 percent of the population. People who buy vitamins tend to be in an upper income group, better educated, and they read a lot." Given this select target market for its product, selecting the right location is a crucial factor in determining each new Vitamin City store's success. To maintain peak efficiency as well as profitability, Herb's strategy is to research prospective locations thoroughly and to "open no more than one new store a year."

Quality

A frequent concern in deciding whether to expand is quality control. The smaller your business, the easier it is for you to spot substandard work or products and take corrective action. Conversely, as your business grows, quality control problems become more difficult to recognize and correct. Hiring a sufficient number of trained managers and workers to handle the increased work load is a step in the right direction for maintaining quality. However, just as too many cooks spoil the broth, they could easily become part of the problem unless their duties are clearly defined and specific quality control guidelines are established.

Service

Like quality, service is an area that often suffers when a business expands. With an increase in size, greeting customers by name or catering to individual needs becomes more difficult. Instead of offering that "something extra" in the way of service, there's a temptation to standardize products and services and treat each customer the same, regardless of his or her special needs.

Because of her desire to provide clients with the best service possible, Alice Byrne is an advocate of slow growth.

Formerly working as a registered nurse, in 1975 she **changed** careers and founded Ambassador Special Ser-**vices, Ltd.**, a New York private investigation and security **guard** business. The same caring and attention to detail **that she** brought to the nursing profession helped to make **her** company one of the top investigative services in the **country.** Explaining her growth policy, Alice says, "I have **always been** conservative in considering expansion in any **area.** I learn first and then train employees on the particu-**lars of** each new account." Whatever the assignment, **whether** it's protecting a store, transporting a valuable **package** or important document, tracing a missing person, **or recovering** a stolen yacht, each of Ambassador's clients **"receives** a very personal service." Following this strategy **has "paid** off," says Alice, adding that in keeping with **Ambassador's** emphasis on service, "I have never accepted **two new** accounts at the same time."

Control

One of the characteristics of a small business is the owner's **ability to** exercise virtually total control over all aspects of **its operation.** The larger the business becomes, generally **the more** complex the control process becomes, with the **power to** make decisions spread out over layers of manage-**ment,** separate product lines, and locations. Thus, in de-**termining** the ideal size for your business, it's important to **determine** the amount of control you wish to retain.

Doug Stephen says, "Many times a business outgrows the **owner** because the business wants to grow but the owner **doesn't.**" Referring to his own business, Modern Fasteners, **Inc., a** distributor of specialty fasteners for industry, he **states,** "At the size of my company, I *run* Modern Fas-**teners.** That's not from an ego position. That's just reality. **But I** have an inside sales manager, an outside sales **manager,** a warehouse manager, and a combined accountant-office manager, so I am starting to delegate and leave more of the day-to-day details to others." However, in developing an expansion policy and turning more decisions over to his staff, Doug makes clear that he's still in control. "I'm not ready to say, 'Here's my company. Take it and run.' It's my company and I'm going to guide and direct it."

Personal Satisfaction

Another factor, less measurable but no less important than the others, is personal satisfaction. In weighing the pros and cons of further expansion, one of the questions you should ask yourself is, "What size business can provide me with the greatest personal satisfaction?" If you enjoy having direct contact with employees and customers, the decision to expand your business might actually decrease your level of personal satisfaction by making it more difficult to maintain this interaction. On the other hand, if you prefer to be involved in long-range planning and policy-making rather than the day-to-day activities of running your business, then developing a large organization with specialists in each area is probably right for you.

Ways to Expand Your Business

After evaluating the preceding factors, if you decide to expand your business, you then need to decide the form that the expansion will take. As the following chart shows, there are several ways to increase the size of your business.

Productivity

One way to expand your business is to increase its productivity and use your existing resources to serve a greater number of customers. Streamlining your procedures, using a computer wherever applicable, and providing employees with additional training are just some of the ways to increase your capacity without physically expanding the size of your business or adding employees. The best part about this method is that it costs the least and can be accomplished in the shortest amount of time.

Product Line

Rather than making more of the same product, expanding your product line increases the size of your business by creating something new. This enables you to reach new customers or sell to your existing customers—again. Doug Stephen doesn't offer customers just one fastener to choose from. His company, Modern Fasteners, Inc., offers a broad range of products from the simplest cable ties up to complete machinery fastening systems for the assembly line. This is the same philosophy followed by the major soap companies, that sell more soaps and detergents by making them available in a variety of forms: for dishes, laundry, face and hands, shampoo, and so on. Depending

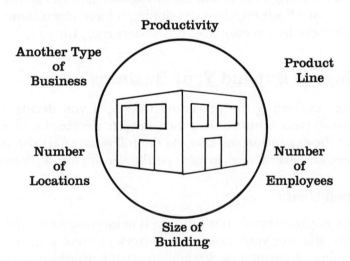

WAYS TO EXPAND YOUR BUSINESS

on the equipment and personnel needed, this method may or may not require physical expansion or additional employees.

Number of Employees

Expanding your business by adding more full-time or part-time employees requires you to expand your resources but doesn't involve capital expenditures. In following this strategy, your goal is to serve your current customers better or to accommodate new ones. For instance, customers, instead of waiting in line or being placed on hold when they phone, will be able to get through to someone who can help them.

Size of Building

If your current location is already bursting at the seams and unable to handle more customers or employees, an alternative is to expand the size of your building. This option depends, of course, on the availability of affordable space in which to expand. Since this method involves capital expenditures and adds to your fixed overhead, look into it closely before going ahead.

Number of Locations

Rather than expanding the size of your current location to meet the growing demand for your product or service, you may decide to increase the number of your locations. Involving both capital expenditures and an increase in your fixed overhead, this type of expansion has several variations. For one, you might want to set up a separate warehouse so that the majority of your existing space can be used for selling and administrative duties. Another variation is to have a separate headquarters office for your administrative activities and a separate showroom or selling office for sales activities. In a third variation, known as a "horizontal combination," a business establishes a chain of locations, with each location offering the same products and services.

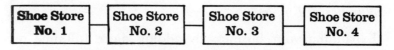

HORIZONTAL COMBINATION

This method of expansion has been particularly successful for grocery and retail stores, restaurants, drugstores, hotels, and motels. However, given the costs of a horizontal combination strategy and its dependence on selecting the right locations, you must allow adequate time to research it.

Another Type of Business

The most complicated and generally costly method of expansion is to branch out into another type of business. Much like expanding your product line, this approach involves creating something new. Only in this case, instead of a new product, it's a new business. One way to do this is to form a "vertical combination." This means expanding your business to encompass the production or distribution activities that are related to it but currently performed by others.

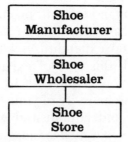

VERTICAL COMBINATION

In the example shown, the owner of the shoe store not only sells shoes, but manufactures and wholesales them as well. A combination like this can originate from the bottom up, from the top down, or even from the middle. Thus the retailer could start the manufacturing plant to guarantee a supply of shoes for the shoe store; the manufacturer could open the shoe store to provide a retail outlet for its shoes; or the wholesaler could expand in both directions to take over the entire production-distribution process.

Another way to branch out into a different type of business is to form a "conglomerate"—a combination of unrelated businesses such as a shoe store, an art gallery, and a textiles plant. Although most closely associated with big business, this method could be employed by smaller businesses seeking to enter new fields. This type of expansion is probably the riskiest of those described since, in addition to its cost, it entails becoming proficient in more than one industry. However, since this strategy allows you to put your eggs in more than one basket, it also can reduce your risk when profits in one area are down.

Considering the various ways to expand your business, you could conceivably select one or all of them. Naturally, if you increase the number of your locations or branch out into other types of business, the number of employees you need also increases. In expanding your product line it may be necessary to expand the size of your building as well, to provide additional manufacturing or selling space. In other words, the decision to expand in one area may require you to expand in another area, too. Like the turns of a Rubik's Cube, each method of expansion affects the others.

The Expansion Rate

Just as important as your method of expansion is your rate of expansion. How fast do you want your business to grow?

According to Doug McDonald, Planning Counselors, Incorporated has been fortunate in that it has been able to "tool up first and then grow into it. If you don't have the money, you have to tool up as you grow." Becoming successful has meant that PCI could set its own expansion rate. "We had people already trained to take on the business before we had it," Doug points out. "That made us very successful because most people were trying to grow companywise and business volumewise at the same time. We grew companywise first." Then, when the number of customer accounts rose, "they could be handled very competently. That made us look good in the marketplace"—and led to even more accounts.

In determining an expansion rate, Doug says business owners should keep in mind that businesses reach "plateaus." "In our business, with a very small group of people, maybe three or four, you can run 200 to 250 pension plans. You can get right up to that point and be profitable, fairly comfortable, and you're not working weekends and nights. The next jump, however, may not just double but triple the people you need. Rather than having three people who do a little bit of everything, all of a sudden you have to begin to specialize."

PCI has reached the point, says Doug, "where I've had to get used to the fact that there are people on staff I don't really know. Now I sign some of those checks and I think, 'Golly, who is this guy?' " As far as the company's current expansion rate is concerned, "What we're evaluating now is 'Do we stay at this point and get very efficient and profitable and enjoy it from that aspect?' or 'Do we make a decision to go bigger?' " If the company decides to expand further, Doug is "concerned that maybe there's a maximum size to this business. We may not be able to go beyond that size without making extraordinary changes—going public or merging with a computer company because a lot of our stuff needs to be computerized. I don't know if we could do that on our own. Trying to do it might break us."

In evaluating what expansion rate is best for your business, the evaluation process should also take into consideration the right rate for you.

When asked the question "How fast do you want your business to grow?" Doug Stephen of Modern Fasteners, Inc. used to answer that he wanted his business to grow as large and as fast as it possibly could. "That was my salesman's answer," he says, the answer that was expected from him, the one people wanted to hear. Today he gives a different answer. "Now I start looking at goals." Having built his business into a successful operation, Doug's strategy is to have its future growth parallel his own personal development.

Elaborating on this expansion strategy, Doug says, "In the next ten years I'm going to be building the business on a continual growth basis. The first priority is not sales dollars growth; it is profit growth." Doug's goal during this period is "to work the next ten years for myself. That's for the personal gratification of Doug Stephen—the ego satisfaction, growth, and all the things that come." At the end of that period, "I'll be fifty-five and I'll say, 'Well, what do I want from life?' The things that I wanted at thirty-five are different than I want at forty-five. At fifty-five, or that range, if I can get my children involved, then I will help them grow and will be leaving them an estate. I'll be leaving them a business, an income." However, if the children choose not to enter the business, then "I'll have to be looking at estate planning. That means I'm now fifty-five and I don't want to really leave the business, but I'm not going to give someone power of attorney to run it." At that point, the expansion rate of his business would slow down considerably. Rather than continuing to build Modern Fasteners, Doug says, "for the next three to five years, I may say that I'm going to take from the business. Then, around sixty, I've got to make a decision. If my children aren't involved, I have to sell the business. And, if I can't sell it, then I basically have to just take from it."

So, as Doug sees it, determining the expansion rate for your business or answering the question "What's the perfect size?" calls for more than a "salesman's answer." The most important thing to ask yourself, in his opinion, is, "What do you want to do?" Another thing to remember, he says, is that your own needs change, too.

3 The Franchise Dilemma

A Fast Track to Riches, or a Costly Detour?

FRANCHISING can provide the influx of capital and people necessary to turn a small business into a giant operation. But if you aren't careful, it can also be the undoing of an already successful business, undermining the consistency and quality of your products or services. Whether franchising is the way to go depends on the individual characteristics of each business—and each business owner.

Making the decision to franchise their self-service salad bar restaurant, The Lettuce Patch, enabled Lois and Elliot Schindel to bring in not only more capital but also dedicated people. "It was just not physically possible for us to do everything," says Lois. Outlining their initial plan, Elliot explains that The Lettuce Patch was really supposed to be "a restaurant for Lois. She would run it. She would operate it and I would come in maybe in the evenings or on weekends. I would still maintain my job [with Litton Industries]. And, maybe in ten or fifteen years, if it caught on, we'd have a little Mom-and-Pop thing going." But it didn't work out that way. "From the moment we put the sign in the window, saying we were open, this place took off," says Elliot. "Seven months later I had to quit Litton because this got too big."

Since that time, Elliot and Lois have opened Lettuce Patch franchises throughout Southern California and are in the process of spreading across the Sunbelt. The restaurant's rapid growth stems in part from the public's heightened awareness of nutrition and the trend toward eating lighter, healthier meals. "We are where McDonald's was twenty years ago," says Elliot. "We have what we call the 'Now foods.' Doctors, schools, health people, dieticians are all preaching get away from meats, get away from fats, get away from oils, and go to the more natural foods. So we're right at the right time."

In addition to timing, Lois believes that much of their success is due to the franchisees themselves. "You have to give credit to the franchisees. They've come to you for your expertise, and that's what they've paid you for. However, they're entrepreneurs, as you are. You've got to look at them as hardworking, bright people who have a vision. They see what you see, a new trend. . . . So you have to listen to the franchisee." This ability to work together—the franchisor with the franchisee—to achieve a common goal has made it possible for The Lettuce Patch to meet the increasing demand for its product.

Despite the advantages franchising may have to offer, Annie Hurlbut is emphatic in saying that it isn't for The Peruvian Connection. She feels that franchising is "antithetical to our company's image of personal service, as well as exclusive merchandise," and she perfers to remain in direct contact with her customers. "Our imported alpaca collection is available only through our mail-order catalogue," says Annie. "We are the only U.S. mail-order firm specializing in this soft, luxury fiber. Most of the sweaters are handmade exclusively for us in Peru. And our unusual gift items are not available in any other North American stores."

In order to maintain the quality of her company's products, Annie and her mother, Biddy, who's also a partner in the business, control all marketing efforts. Says Annie, "The result is a handmade collection we're proud to back with an ironclad, moneyback guarantee. You can count on us for direct, friendly service." In Annie's view, this claim would not be possible if The Peruvian Connection were operated as a franchise. "We see our roles as *direct* market-ers [rather than as franchisors]," she states. "Long-term, it's better value for our customers."

Is Franchising Right for Me?

Franchising, though commonly associated with the fast-food industry, has proven its applicability to a number of other areas as well. Currently, as shown in the accompany-ing chart, franchising accounts for 34 percent of all U.S. retail sales.

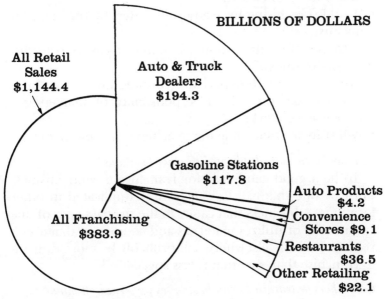

BILLIONS OF DOLLARS

All Retail Sales $1,144.4

Auto & Truck Dealers $194.3

Gasoline Stations $117.8

Auto Products $4.2

Convenience Stores $9.1

Restaurants $36.5

Other Retailing $22.1

All Franchising $383.9

Source: U.S. Department of Commerce

FRANCHISING ENCOMPASSED 34% OF RETAIL SALES IN 1982

Long a standard method of doing business in the automobile and oil industries, franchising now can be found in such diverse fields as print shops, physical fitness centers, real-estate brokerages, florist shops, bookstores, beauty salons, and motels. In recent years even the medical and legal professions have succumbed to franchising's lure.

Given this popularity, you may wonder, "Is franchising right for me?" To evaluate whether franchising is suitable for your business, first examine the business itself. Start by asking yourself:

- Can my business be duplicated in other locations?
- Can others be trained to run businesses patterned on mine?
- Is it economically feasible to franchise my business?
- Can adequate controls be enforced to protect my business if it is franchised?
- Would franchising have a positive effect on the image of my business?
- Is there sufficient customer demand to justify franchising my business?
- Do I have enough experience running my current business to take the added responsibility of managing a franchise network?
- Will franchising enable me to achieve my objectives?

Can my business be duplicated in other locations?

To be a good candidate for franchising, your business must be one that can be successfully duplicated in other locations. A business that caters to the special needs of one community or utilizes materials and equipment that aren't readily available elsewhere will probably be more difficult to franchise than one that is less specialized.

Can others be trained to run businesses patterned on mine?

The greater the amount of education, skills, or experience required to run your business, the harder it will be to franchise it. It's easier to train someone to run a restaurant or change an automobile muffler than to train someone to create an original artwork or program a computer.

Is it economically feasible to franchise my business?

In the beginning,the costs of meeting state and federal regulations, preparing contracts, registering patents or trademarks, advertising, training franchisees, and traveling from one franchise location to another can easily equal or surpass the revenues from your original business. It's important for you to have a solid financial base from which to expand.

Can adequate controls be enforced to protect my business if it is franchised?

Since the actions of one franchisee reflect on all the others, maintaining adequate control over the entire franchise operation is crucial to your success. Your business must lend itself to standardized procedures and policies that can be enforced for the good of all franchise members.

Would franchising have a positive effect on the image of my business?

In considering franchising's effect on your business operation, also consider its effect on your company's image. If your business is known for its one-of-a-kind products or personalized service, franchising's broader marketing approach might detract from that image of exclusivity.

Is there sufficient customer demand to justify franchising my business?

Increasing the size of your operation through franchising calls for increasing your customer base as well. It's important to determine in advance if the potential demand for your product or service is large enough to support a franchise network.

Do I have enough experience running my current business to take on the added responsibility of managing a franchise network?

Business owners in a hurry to capitalize on a hot idea or get the jump on the competition sometimes rush into franchising before they are ready for it, often with disastrous results. It's a good idea to wait until you have had enough time to get used to running your existing business before taking on others.

Will franchising enable me to achieve my objectives?

Developing a franchise network is time-consuming, costly, and requires a great deal of commitment on the part of the franchisor. Before deciding to franchise your business, ask yourself if this method is compatible with your objectives—both professionally and personally.

Carol Brothers, founder of POP-INS, Inc., a maid service and carpet cleaning franchise, was able to say yes to each of the preceding questions. As a result, the business she started in 1977 is now one of the fastest-growing franchisors in the nation.

Like other successful businesses, POP-INS was created to fill a need. In this case, Carol says, it was "my own need. I was an interior decorator and wanted my own house to look beautiful and clean." However, after devoting time to her career and family, Carol found that there wasn't much time left to do housework. "I needed help," she recalls. So she decided to hire a part-time maid.

"After the hassle of interviewing fourteen women and checking references, I finally found someone," Carol says. That's when the trouble began. "When I told my accountant about the housekeeper, he informed me that I was required to obtain an employer identification number, withhold federal and state taxes, pay Social Security, Workers Compensation, and a special liability insurance . . . all for a part-time maid." Carol thought, "There must be an easier way. Wouldn't it be wonderful just to pick up the telephone and have a team of maids miraculously appear and clean my home from one end to the other, then leave? There must be a way to get my home cleaned without all this hassle." At this point the idea for POP-INS was born.

Thirteen months after starting her business, Carol sold her first POP-INS franchise. The decision to franchise was a major one, which came about when Carol had reached the turning point. She could continue to run a small, successful business or try to go nationwide, even international. On the strength of her company's financial statements, she chose to do the latter.

Since her decision to franchise, POP-INS has expanded across the United States and is now establishing franchises in Europe. The company's rapid growth, not surprisingly, has paralleled the increase in the number of working women. "With both the husband and wife working," Carol points out, "no way do they want to come home and clean house."

Franchising has not only helped POP-INS to grow but also has enabled the company to create a positive image for itself, while at the same time improving the image of domestic work. "Before the POP-INS concept," Carol explains, "there were a lot of problems with maid service. Many thought of it as demeaning work. We've taken that area and given it class. Each of our maids drives a new car to work, has a partner, and works on commission. I guess you could say we've upgraded the image of the housekeeper. My workers are screened. They're trained experts. They're covered by half-a-million dollars' worth of liability insurance. They're bonded. Their work is guaranteed. If the work doesn't suit a customer or client, the technicians have to come back and do it again . . . at no charge."

In order to ensure that her high standards are met, Carol provides each franchisee with training both at the new franchise location and at the company's headquarters in Columbiana, Ohio. Video training casettes, a telephone hot line for on-the-spot questions, a company newsletter, and visits from POP-INS home office representatives fill out the training program. For their part, as stated in the "master franchise concept," franchisees are expected to "administer POP-INS policies, procedures, and uniformity standards; maintain quality control; equipment, and supply control; and assist with collections."

"Owning my own business has a lot of rewards," Carol

says. "It is wonderful to see an idea become a little business, grow into a franchise, then into an international company. That's exciting." In addition to achieving her own objectives through POP-INS, Carol is pleased to be in a position to help others achieve their objectives, too. "We're helping a lot of people make their dreams come true, to become the proud owners of their own profitable business."

In debating whether or not franchising would be right for Wordplay, the do-it-yourself word processing center he helped start, Peter Van den Beemt says, "It would be nice to be the McDonald's of word processing. Unfortunately, so far, the skill level of the people running our business has to be a lot greater than the skill level of the people running McDonald's. Contrary to what people may think, the computer doesn't do all the work." Adds partner Bob Dietz, "We've discovered that this is a much more labor-intensive business than we realized." Compounding the problem of franchising their business is the fact that the quality of their work must meet exceedingly high standards. "The public is *so* demanding," says partner Michele Palmer. "Sometimes it's like having nine six-year-olds out there going, 'Mommy! Daddy!' "

To maintain this level of quality and get additional practice in the management aspects of the business, Bob says, "We might end up opening a branch someplace just to go through the experience of doing it. Then we'd learn about what needs to be done because we'd have to start all over again from scratch. That would be a good way to start out." Michele and Peter agree that establishing a second Wordplay outlet is probably the best approach—for now. But, although all three partners believe that franchising their business is a definite possibility, it's still a ways off. "At the moment, we don't feel we know enough to know how to do it," says Peter. "We don't know enough to tell people, 'Here's the system. Here's the rule book. You can open the door.' "

The Legal Side of Franchising

If and when you make the move to franchise your business, it's important that you comply with Federal Trade Commission regulations regarding franchising. In an effort to protect the public, the FTC requires a franchisor to provide any prospective franchisee with a "disclosure statement" revealing the franchisor's background, the financial status of the company, terms of the franchise agreement, and so on. Comprising twenty different subject categories in all, the disclosure statement must furnish the following information:

1. Identification of the franchisor and its affiliates and description of their business experience
2. Identification and description of the business experience of each of the franchisor's officers, directors, and management personnel responsible for franchise services, training, and other aspects of the franchise program
3. Any lawsuits in which the franchisor and its officers, directors, and management personnel have been involved
4. Any previous bankruptcies in which the franchisor and its officers, directors, and management personnel have been involved
5. The initial franchise fee and other initial payments that are required to obtain the franchise
6. The continuing payments franchisees are required to make after the franchise opens
7. Any restrictions on the quality of goods and services used in the franchise and where they may be purchased, including restrictions requiring purchases from the franchisor or its affiliates
8. Any assistance available from the franchisor or its affiliates in financing the purchase of the franchise
9. Restrictions on the goods or services franchises are permitted to sell

10. Any restrictions on the customers with whom franchisees may deal

11. Any territorial protection that will be granted to the franchisee

12. The conditions under which the franchise may be repurchased or refused renewal by the franchisor, transferred to a third party by the franchisee, or terminated or modified by either party

13. The training programs provided to franchisees

14. The involvement of any celebrities or public figures in the franchise

15. Any assistance by the franchisor in selecting a site for the franchise

16. Statistics about the present number of franchises; the number of franchises projected for the future; and the number of franchises terminated, the number the franchisor has decided not to renew, and the number repurchased in the past

17. Financial statements of the franchisors

18. The extent to which franchisees must personally participate in the operation of the franchise

19. A complete statement of the basis for any earnings claim made to the franchisee, including the percentage of existing franchises that have actually achieved the results claimed

20. Names and addresses of other franchisees

In addition to the disclosure statement requirement, the Federal Trade Commission has also taken steps to give prospective franchisees a number of important legal rights under federal law. Thus, for your own protection, it's essential for you to be aware of these rights. In accordance with the FTC's ruling, prospective franchisees have:

1. The right to receive a disclosure statement at their first personal meeting with a representative of the franchisor to discuss the purchase of a franchise, but

in no event less than ten business days before they sign a franchise or related agreement, or pay any money in connection with the purchase of a franchise.

2. The right to receive documentation stating the basis and assumptions for any earnings claims made at the time the claims are made, but in no event less than ten business days before they sign a franchise or related agreement, or pay any money in connection with the purchase of a franchise. If an earnings claim is made in advertising, they have the right to receive the required documentation at their first personal meeting with a representative of the franchisor.

3. The right to receive sample copies of the franchisor's standard franchise and related agreements at the same time they receive the disclosure statement, and the right to receive the final agreements they are to sign at least five business days before they sign them.

4. The right to receive any refunds promised by the franchisor, subject to any conditions or limitations on that right that have been disclosed by the franchisor.

5. The right not to be misled by oral or written representations that are inconsistent with the disclosures made in the disclosure statement.

If a franchisor is found to be in violation of federal law, the Federal Trade Commission is authorized to levy a penalty against the offender. What's more, if a prospective franchisee is able to prove that he or she has been injured by the franchisor's action, the franchisor may also be required to compensate the individual for any money lost and rescind the existing franchise agreement.

As a franchisor, to protect yourself against possible lawsuits, before attempting to put together a disclosure statement or negotiate with prospective franchisees, first consult both an attorney and a certified public accountant. In that way you can find out what procedures to follow to keep your franchise operation legal, as well as the cost of developing the franchise package that will be offered to investors.

The International Franchise Association Code of Ethics

To improve the image of franchising in general and relations between franchisors and franchisees in particular, the International Franchise Association, a nonprofit association of franchisors, has developed a Code of Ethics for its members. To get a better idea of your obligations as a franchisor and determine the effect of franchising on your business, you may wish to examine this code.

According to the Code of Ethics, each member company pledges that:

1. No member shall offer, sell, or promote the sale of any franchise, product, or service by means of any explicit or implied representation that is likely to have a tendency to deceive or mislead prospective purchasers of such franchise, product, or service.
2. No member shall imitate the trademark, trade name, corporate name, slogan, or other mark of identification of another business in any manner or form that would have the tendency or capacity to mislead or deceive.
3. The pyramid or chain distribution system in inimical to prospective investors and to the franchise system of distribution, and no member shall engage in any form of pyramid or chain distribution.
4. An advertisement, considered in its totality, shall be free from ambiguity and, in whatever form presented, must be considered in its entirety and as it would be read and understood by those to whom directed.

5. All advertisements shall comply, in letter and spirit, with all applicable rules, regulations, directives, guides, and laws promulgated by any government body or agency having jurisdiction.

6. An advertisement containing or making reference, directly or indirectly, to performance records, figures, or data respecting income or earnings of franchisees shall be factual and, if necessary to avoid deception, accurately qualified as to geographical area and time periods covered.

7. An advertisement containing information or making reference to the investment requirements of a franchise shall be as detailed as necessary to avoid being misleading in any way and shall be specific with respect to whether the stated amount (or amounts) is a partial or the full cost of the franchise, the items paid for by the stated amount (or amounts), financing requirements, and other related costs.

8. Full and accurate written disclosure of all information considered material to the franchise relationship shall be given to prospective franchisees a reasonable time prior to the execution of any binding document, and members shall otherwise fully comply with federal and state laws requiring advance disclosure of information to prospective franchisees.

9. All matters relative to the franchise relationship shall be contained in one or more written agreements, which shall clearly set forth the terms of the relationship and the respective rights and obligations of the parties.

10. A franchisor shall select and accept only those franchisees who, upon reasonable investigation, appear to possess the basic skills, education, personal qualities, and financial resources adequate to perform and fulfill the needs and requirements of the fran-

chise. There shall be no discrimination based on race, color, religion, or sex.

11. The franchisor shall encourage and/or provide training designed to help franchisees improve their abilities to conduct their franchises.

12. A franchisor shall provide reasonable guidance and supervision over the business activities of franchisees for the purpose of safeguarding the public interest and of maintaining the integrity of the entire franchise system for the benefit of all parties having an interest in it.

13. Fairness shall characterize all dealings between a franchisor and its franchisees. To the extent reasonably appropriate under the circumstances, a franchisor shall give notice to its franchisee of any contractual breach and grant reasonable time to remedy default.

14. A franchisor should be conveniently accessible and responsive to communications from franchisees, and provide a mechanism by which ideas may be exchanged and areas of concern discussed for the purpose of improving mutual understanding and reaffirming mutuality of interest.

15. A franchisor shall make every effort to resolve complaints, grievances, and disputes with its franchisees with good faith and goodwill through fair and reasonable direct communication and negotiation. Failing this, consideration should be given to mediation or arbitration.

4 Replenishing the Soil

Keeping the Vitality in Your Business

ONE of the measures of a successful business is its ability to nurture the creativity and enthusiasm of its people. Whatever means you use to accomplish this—an open-door policy, financial incentives, job training, and so on—the goal is the same: to maintain an environment in which new ideas can flourish and employees can reach their potentials.

Motivating Your Employees

Regardless of the type of business you run or the kinds of duties your employees perform, the success of your business relates directly to your own success as a motivator. The people you rely on to help carry out the functions of your business rely, in turn, on you. As the owner, you are expected to provide leadership and to assist employees in their personal development. In short, you are expected to be a motivator. In the course of interviewing the entrepreneurs selected for our book, a wide variety of motivational strategies became apparent. These include motivating employees by: setting an example; encouraging employee involvement; providing opportunities for career advancement; expressing concern for the employees' well-being;

employing generalists rather than specialists; and selling
stock in the company.

Motivating by Example

Lina Lidow, of Lina Lee, believes that the best way to instill
a feeling of enthusiasm in her employees is through example. "If I don't have it, my sales staff won't have it. There
are days when I come in totally exhausted, when I really
want to say, 'Let's go on vacation. Let's just forget it.' But I
really feel that I am a role model. Because I am an owner-
manager, I'm here every day. I never ask a girl to do
something I wouldn't do myself. Whether it's taking out
the garbage because we're busy, or whatever, I always try
to set the example. I think that if I were detached and not
interested and always giving orders, it would be impossible
to have a motivated staff."

Rather than confining her activities to administration,
Lina makes it a point to be on the sales floor as much as
possible. "I talk to the girls constantly," she says. "We have
staff meetings every morning for forty-five minutes, and
in those meetings I tell the girls everything I know, from
the history of the designer to what the material is. This
includes answering questions such as, 'Why is this blouse
nine hundred dollars?' 'What was the designer's idea in
designing a nine-hundred-dollar blouse?' 'What are the
colors for the season, and why?' 'What do they relate to?'
We go over all these little details because an average outfit
in the store is now two thousand dollars, head-to-toe. You
can get it for less, you can get it for more. But that's an
average sale. My feeling is that if a customer's spending
two thousand dollars or much more, a salesgirl just can't
say, 'Oh, you look beautiful!' And if she's spending sixty
thousand dollars, which is not uncommon, you're with the
customer for four hours. What do you say? 'What does
your husband do? Oh, you look good. I like your hair. Do
you have children?' Well, you run out of things to say, and

a lot of things you can't ask politely. So the girls have to have knowledge and information that a normal salesgirl doesn't have."

Surprisingly enough, half of the people working at Lina Lee have not had any fashion experience. "But," Lina explains, "they're bright and they're quick learners and interested in fashion and interested in clothes. So they're always very observant and they listen and they learn." In addition to this, part of their training takes place in the daily staff meetings where they put together outfits, gather information, and are actually quizzed on it. "One morning I'll give them all the information on [Italian designers] Luciano Soprani or Gianfranco Ferre. The next morning they have to tell it to me back, as though I were a customer. It's fun. I mean, you have to be able to laugh. They're not always serious sessions, obviously, or I'd lose my whole staff."

Encouraging Employee Involvement

The same motivation and training techniques that work in the fashion industry apply just as well in other fields.

Fred Salenger, owner of Salenger Educational Media, an educational products company, says, "We try our best to involve the people and to get suggestions and to be creative. The environment's open. The doors are never closed. We discuss management and business right in the front office. It makes no difference. We have no secrets from anybody. Everybody can contribute."

One of the areas in which employees are particularly encouraged to get involved is in making the management training and motivation films that the company produces and distributes. "We call them in before we even produce a film," says Fred. "They look at the script, read the script. We bounce ideas off of them. A film is true to life. I may see something in it. Somebody else may react to it differently. The more input, the better." Thus, someone from the accounting or shipping department is as likely to make a worthwhile contribution to a film as is any other employee.

Given this free exchange of ideas and a relaxed atmosphere, Salenger Educational Media's employee turnover rate is very low. Obviously pleased by this, Fred's attitude is, "I'm here eight, nine hours a day, even more, physically, and I want it to be like home. We have a lot of pictures on the walls, bright colors, nice carpets. It makes people feel more comfortable. Also, we don't have any time clocks. People are really on the honor system."

The fact that this approach works for him, though, doesn't necessarily mean it would be right for everyone, Fred points out. "Don't forget there are a lot of people who can't work in this environment. Being a small firm, when we choose people, we lay out the whole environment. Because if somebody needs a lot of guidance—like a Theory X [more structured] style of management—it's not going to work for us."

Providing Opportunities for Advancement

Doug McDonald, of Planning Counselors, Incorporated, motivates his employees by offering them opportunities for advancement and profit sharing. He emphasizes that he wants to instill in them "a sense of accomplishment, the feeling that they really are accomplishing something that is technical, that takes some brains, and that is productive." Rather than just asking a secretary to type a letter to a client, he frequently asks the secretary to research and write the letter, as well. This helps to broaden the employee's skills level and prepare him or her for a higher position within the company.

A firm believer in the value of feedback, Doug makes it a point to give employees as much direct contact with the company's clients as possible. "If I don't do that, they [the employees] are not getting any of the good parts—the face-to-face contact, the compliments for the good job that we are doing. They need that positive feedback."

Even when the feedback isn't positive, it still can provide a learning experience. "People can prepare a set of things for me to take out to make a presentation," says Doug. "And the worst feeling in the whole world is to be making the presentation and have the client say, 'On page five here, isn't that a mistake?' That's a very impressive moment. It stays with you for a while." Employees "need to go through that because they're preparing [the materials], and they need to feel how unrecoverable that mistake is." This kind of on-the-job training enables employees to "get the compliments and the criticism both, face to face. It also gives them the opportunity to see that there is advancement."

According to Doug, "One organization located in Washington does training in this field. And that's it. It's not given in the schools. That's been a big problem." As a result, most of the formal training that employees receive takes place in-house, provided either by Doug or the employees themselves. For instance, an employee might be assigned a topic such as "the taxation of distributions" and be asked to report on it to the others in the company. This gives the employee not only the chance to become an expert on that specific topic, but also the chance to gain recognition from his or her peers.

Planning Counselors, Incorporated's commitment to the well-being and advancement of its employees is also demonstrated through its profit-sharing plan. Thus, when the company is doing well, the employees benefit, too. "If we have a good year, we put money in," says Doug, and allow the employees to share in the profits.

Expressing Concern for Employees

Karen York is a partner with Barbara Alpern in the York Group, a business specializing in advertising, public relations, and marketing services. Karen believes that as women business owners, "We do bring a level of concern and caring for our employees that you might not find [otherwise]. I think that we just do it naturally. It's not a matter of thinking about it." Adds Barbara, "When we see that someone is a little withdrawn or moody, we'll let it go the first day, the second day. Maybe it's just something they need to work out. But we won't let it go for very long. We'll go up and call the person in and say, 'What's happening? Is it something personal? Is it something professional? How can we remedy the situation? Let's discuss it.' Because if they're unhappy, then it creates an aura of discomfort for everybody, and we don't allow it to go on."

"The dynamics are so intense here," says Karen. "It's essential to maintain a supportive environment. Everybody here is management; we have no troops here. Everybody really handles a specific area of the business." To develop a feeling of *esprit de corps* and enhance the team effort, both partners stress that employees need "to feel a part of what's going on here and to get the creative kick that we get by producing a good product." So, when Karen and Barbara are preparing to give a presentation, they make it a point to get everybody participating and to solicit everybody's input. As Karen describes it, "We'll say in our production meetings, 'This opportunity has been made available to us, and this is the kind of information that we'll need, and this is what the client shared with me, and I'd like to organize it this way.' " Then the meeting is thrown open for suggestions, which usually aren't long in coming. In Karen's words, "Everybody just opens their mouth here. It's not a real chain of command."

In dealing with their employees, Karen and Barbara both feel that it's important to be honest with them. In this regard, the employees "do know what's going on," says Barbara. "We tell them when times are rough. We tell them when we're up against really tight deadlines. We tell them about some of the pressures that clients are putting on us.

They are really very much involved in what's happening in the business." Thus, when the employees are told that there is a deadline to meet, they *know* that it's not just a ploy to get extra productivity out of them. Nevertheless, Karen says with a laugh, "They often accuse us of having the same deadline for every client."

The York Group also shows its concern for the employees' personal development. Employees are encouraged to attend professional seminars to improve their skills or gain business-related information. "Whenever something appropriate comes along, I'll urge them to participate," says Karen. "And I'll pay for it. I'm not going to send them to Hawaii, or something. But if I feel that there is an area that we could both benefit from—them and the agency—then I will underwrite it."

Employing Generalists

"There are always two theories," says Dorothy Beam, owner of her own travel agency, Signal Travel Services. You can "be a specialist or a generalist. Well, I think in an agency, if you specialize and you just sit on that phone and all you do is commercial accounts, you're going to get burnout. People like variety. I think it's more stimulating. Well, obviously it keeps their interest. There is so much to learn."

What's more, Dorothy contends, a generalist approach is not only good for the individuals but for the agency, too. "In the travel business you almost always have someone traveling. That's the name of the game. So who's going to do that someone's job if there aren't others in the office who know it just as well?" Given this need to rotate work assignments and fill in the gaps left by traveling employees, Dorothy believes that specializing would be less efficient. Yet, she points out, many agencies do. "Agencies tell me, 'We have people who specialize. That's all they do.' When they're gone someone else has to step in. But what's happening to somebody else's job when they're stepping in and doing that? So my people do everything."

When it comes to motivating her employees, Dorothy says, "As far as I'm concerned, the first requirement is a pleasant working atmosphere—comfortable, with everything you need to work with. I give general guidelines, but within those guidelines *you* do it the way it works for you. I'm not going to *tell* you how to write. I want complete records, but I want you to do it in the way that's the most comfortable for you." Thus, rather than feeling boxed in or that their creativity is being stifled, employees feel that their jobs can be what they make them to be. This is the way Dorothy wants them to feel. "A lot of people who work in the travel industry, who work for the tour operators or the airlines, are in such regimented, compartmentalized types of jobs that they really don't like them very well. They're really quite bored. And, believe me, it sure comes through." In such instances, she says, they won't go that "second step" to please the customer.

"We work hard, but we play hard, too," says Dorothy. "We have a refrigerator, a lunch area, a microwave. We bring in champagne quite frequently. A lot of times we have clients in and we open champagne and relax and have a good time. So I think that the general atmosphere is a nice one." In addition, Dorothy provides employees with the opportunity to take "familiarization trips" each year to the various places where they are sending their clients. As for providing financial incentives, Dorothy doesn't overlook these either. Employees receive two weeks' vacation and medical benefits, says Dorothy, along with salaries that are "in line with, or higher than, those at other travel agencies."

Selling Stock in your Company

Another way to sell your employees on your business is literally to sell them the business, or a part of it.

Richard LaMotta insists that every employee buy stock in Chipwich, Inc. Explaining the reason for this, he says, "I knew I was going to work eighty to a hundred hours a week and I said, 'The only way you're going to do that is if you own a piece of the company and if you have a shot at becoming fairly wealthy from this.' So I made everybody have shares in it. I said, 'You're not working here unless you buy shares!' I didn't want a lot of money. I wasn't saying, 'You have to fund the business.' But I knew that an employee who had a thousand shares of my company wasn't going to be complaining about a forty-hour work-week."

Richard not only requires employees to invest in the company but to be "entrepreneurial-minded" as well. His street vendors are trained to become "entrepreneurs of their own small business—the vending cart." To maintain the company's high-quality image and to generate sales, each Chipwich vendor is carefully screened from many applicants before being selected to sell the chocolate chip cookie and ice-cream treats. Once selected, the vendor's schooling includes a comprehensive program of classroom seminars and on-the-job training.

Beyond having dedication and good entrepreneurial skills, Richard looks for enthusiasm in his workers. "You can see that gleam. You can tell that enthusiasm when they come in to look for a job. And, unless they have it, I don't want them around. I only want people who are positive thinkers." To attract and hold onto high-caliber employees, Richard's strategy is simple: "I try to pay liberally and I reward people and I infuse a very positive image, one of affirmation in the company. Here's what we are doing and why we're different and why we're successful and here's what's happening. We are writing one of the greatest success stories."

Motivating Yourself

Jut as important as the need to motivate your employees is the need to motivate yourself. It's not uncommon for business owners to get so caught up in the motivational needs of their employees that they end up overlooking their own. During the start-up phase of a business this doesn't pose much of a problem. The challenge of just getting started is motivation enough. But once the initial excitement wears off, it's important to discover new ways to maintain your energy level and enthusiasm.

Does running your business still give you the same feeling of satisfaction that you felt in the beginning? Do you approach each day with a sense of exhilaration and purpose? Or, having achieved your goal of success, is the thrill of accomplishment suddenly harder to find? Has invention given way to routine? Brainstorming to bureaucracy? Under these circumstances, more than one business owner has made the same fatal mistake—accepting success as a permanent condition rather than a temporary one that must be maintained. To keep the vitality in your business, first keep the vitality in yourself.

Learning as a Motivator

The act of learning itself is a motivator for Lina Lidow. "I'd always wanted to have my own business," she says. "I like the challenge. I like competition. And I've always been a hard worker. Long hours don't really bother me. Being able to see immediately whether you're successful or not, to see your mistakes, to see your good points, I like that. And being your own boss, being able to say, 'Now I can change it,' or, 'This is my fault because it happened this way and next time I'll know better.' One of the things I like about business is learning . . . and learning quickly . . . and learning from experience, as opposed to learning through others."

The Challenge to Succeed

"You're never comfortable" in this business, says Fred Salenger. Because "if you get too relaxed, you can let it slip through pretty fast." Given fluctuations in economy and changes in customer needs, it's a constant challenge to stay on top of things. "The recession is a perfect example of this," points out Fred. "You're going along making a profit. All of a sudden there are external situations you have no control over. If you're not fast to react to those situations, you can go under very fast. So you're never really relaxed."

Unlike companies that produce the same products over and over again in vast quantities, Salenger Educational Media's products are all unique. Thus, in addition to the challenge of running his business, Fred is also motivated by the challenge to create new products. "This is a guessing game," he says. "We produce a film and there's a fifty-fifty chance of making money on it. Every film is different. Every product is different. If you guess right the majority of the time, you're okay."

Problem-Solving

The satisfaction he gets in discovering new ways to solve his clients' problems provides Doug McDonald with a continual source of motivation. The thrill comes, he says, from "grappling with a problem and coming up with something that I'm really excited to take out to the client. If you hit it, that's a real glorious moment."

Echoing that statement are Karen York and Barbara Alpern. "The aspects about this business that I love the most," says Barbara, "are finding the problem and coming up with a solution that's different and fresh and that we created." When this happens, "We just chortle over it," adds Karen. To her, nothing's more exhilarating than "just sitting down to write some copy and out of nothing comes an idea."

Gaining Control

On the subject of self-motivation, Dorothy Beam says, "There's no problem there. There is so much to do. I love the business. I love what I'm doing. I love being my own boss. I love having control over my life. Even though I have stress, even though I have all these other pressures, I am in control of what I do. I like that."

The Freedom to Create

"It's easy to generate energy when it's exciting," says Richard LaMotta. "There seems to be something new happening every day." Best of all, given the number of companies and individuals who are eager to jump on the Chipwich bandwagon, now he can focus on being creative rather than trying to raise money. This wasn't always the case. "I always had trouble finding money," he says. "I always went into business underfinanced. I didn't have the wherewithal to really make it big. Now, all of a sudden, people are saying to me, 'Please, whatever you do next, we want in.' It's hard not to get buoyed up by that!"

Maintaining High Morale

Given how low morale can damage a business, it's essential that you be able to recognize it and take appropriate action. This isn't always easy. Unlike sales volume or the amount of money paid out in commissions, morale cannot be directly measured. Since it's a state of mind, or attitude, rather than a physical condition, morale can only be measured indirectly. Thus, to determine the level (high or low) of your employees' morale, you must observe their behavior.

When workers feel good about themselves and the work they do, employee morale is bound to be high. In this situation your business benefits. When workers feel they are being taken advantage of or that the work they do is unimportant, employee morale is bound to be low. In this instance your business suffers. The following chart indicates some signs of low morale among employees:

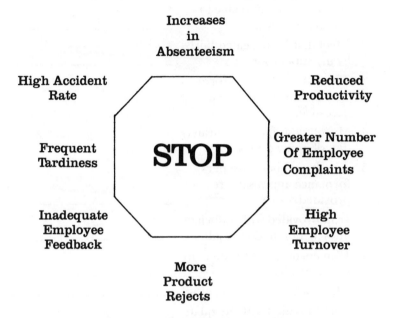

**Increases
in
Absenteeism**

**High Accident
Rate**

**Reduced
Productivity**

**Frequent
Tardiness**

STOP

**Greater Number
Of Employee
Complaints**

**Inadequate
Employee
Feedback**

**High
Employee
Turnover**

**More
Product
Rejects**

WARNING SIGNS OF LOW MORALE

By being alert to these behavior signs, you can readily measure the level of employee morale. However, measuring it and changing it are two different things. In the event that low morale is detected, in order to correct it, you must also determine what *problems* are causing it. Do employees feel overworked? Underpaid? Unappreciated? Are there personality conflicts or scheduling problems? Is the work environment itself considered to be positive, or negative?

To answer these questions and more, ask your employees to fill out a questionnaire similar to the one that follows. Based on the individual circumstances of your business, you may wish to add or delete questions.

EMPLOYEE SATISFACTION QUESTIONNAIRE

	Usually	Sometimes	Never
1. In achieving the goals of the company I am also able to achieve my own.	_____	_____	_____
2. I feel that I am treated fairly by my supervisor.	_____	_____	_____
3. The standards of performance set for my job are not excessive.	_____	_____	_____
4. My job description accurately describes my duties.	_____	_____	_____
5. Timely and objective performance appraisals are provided.	_____	_____	_____
6. I am provided with sufficient information to do my job.	_____	_____	_____
7. I am encouraged to come up with new ideas.	_____	_____	_____
8. The work I do is stimulating.	_____	_____	_____
9. I am provided with adequate working conditions.	_____	_____	_____
10. I feel that I am adequately paid.	_____	_____	_____
11. The deadlines and job pressures are manageable and within reason.	_____	_____	_____
12. Additional training is available to me.	_____	_____	_____
13. The company makes it a point to promote qualified employees.	_____	_____	_____
14. The fringe benefits I receive compare favorably with those provided by other companies.	_____	_____	_____

Employee Satisfaction Questionnaire, Cont'd

	Usually	Sometimes	Never
15. I am appreciated by the company.	_____	_____	_____
16. I feel secure in my job.	_____	_____	_____
17. I take pride in the work I do.	_____	_____	_____
18. The company keeps me informed on matters that affect me.	_____	_____	_____
19. Employee complaints are dealt with quickly and fairly.	_____	_____	_____
20. I have an opportunity to participate in the decision-making process.	_____	_____	_____
21. Employees at all levels in the company work together as a team.	_____	_____	_____
22. Employees generally like working for the company.	_____	_____	_____

Once you have the questionnaires back, you'll be in a good position to identify any underlying problems that exist and work to reduce or eliminate them. In so doing, you'll be on your way to maintaining high employee morale.

5 Grain or Chaff

Recognizing Opportunities When You See Them

HAVING built your business into a successful operation, you may be tempted to keep things the way they are, staying with the same products and services or marketing methods rather than exploring new possibilities. However, playing it safe often proves a more dangerous strategy than venturing into unknown territory. To compete effectively in the marketplace, business owners must constantly be on the lookout for those new ideas or better ways of doing things that can improve their businesses or even revolutionize an industry.

It also helps if you know how to "turn negatives into positives," says entrepreneur Marie Vega. After she developed hypoglycemia, she became interested in the health aspects of beauty care and went on to develop an entirely new approach to beauty—a totally natural and healthy way to look and feel good. Dubbed by many as "the Vega look," her system emphasizes the physical and psychological aspects of beauty care rather than the cosmetic. "I've stopped with the blow dryers and the hair colors and the permanents and all of that," Marie says vehemently.

She's aware that her program goes against the grain of the beauty industry. "I'm the only one who does it." Rather than enhancing the body's natural beauty, the trend in the beauty industry has been to camouflage or change it to meet artificial standards, she contends. "We've all been brainwashed. You can't walk outside unless you have a coat of veneer to cover up the real you. What is wrong with gray hair? If you have inner beauty, you will always be young regardless of your hair color."

Marie advises her clients to cut down on their intake of coffee, sugar, salt, soft drinks, and wine, while eliminating smoking altogether. "Just by looking at someone's hair you can tell they have bad habits and are eating the wrong things," Marie points out. Firm in her belief that "people are totally killing themselves" with both the things they put into their bodies and on them, Marie is using her knowledge of health not only to change the public's perception of beauty but also to change the beauty industry itself.

Researching the Market

To ensure that your business is fully utilizing its resources and not missing out on desirable opportunities, look both to the past and the future. First look to the past, determine your business strengths and weaknesses, then try to predict which trends or changes in consumer demand you can capitalize on. By taking the time to research the market in this way, you may discover that a previously strong product or service is becoming obsolete because of technological advances or changes in customer needs. On the other hand, a little-noticed product or service may actually be growing in popularity, possibly for the very same reasons. For example, sales of typewriters may be dropping off while sales of word processors are increasing.

Sources of Marketing Information

One of the greatest needs of business owners today is for accurate and current information on which to base their marketing decisions. Who are your customers? Where are they? Why do they buy? How often do they buy? How much do they spend? What sizes, colors, shapes, styles, or flavors do they prefer? Is the demand for your products or services rising or falling? Who is your competition? What effect does the economy have on your business? What new customers or markets can you reach? Knowing the answers to these questions and more is the key to capitalizing on new opportunities.

Although researching the market may sound difficult, costly, and time-consuming, it's a lot easier than it seems. What's more, most of the information you need is already in your possession or can be readily acquired. Your best sources of marketing information include your business records, customers, salespeople, suppliers, and trade associations, as well as government and the media.

Business Records

In addition to monitoring your business' income statement and balance sheet figures, also keep close tabs on your sales records, noting the revenues and expenses by product, product line, type of service, sales territory (or store), and so on. This not only enables you to determine what your sales level is, but also *why*. Do some products move faster than others? Which products aren't moving at all? Are certain colors or styles more in demand than they were last year? Are selling costs for a particular product or service rising faster than the corresponding profits?

Customers

Paying attention to customers' shopping habits and buying patterns is one way to gather marketing information. This can be accomplished by observation, surveys, or questionnaires. Another way, which is being used more frequently by businesses, is to conduct "focus group sessions." In these sessions customers (usually from five to fifteen in number) talk about their individual needs and attitudes in relation to the business' products or services. Focus group sessions can be particularly useful in providing feedback about the image of your company, the competence and friendliness of personnel, the value of what your business has to offer in comparison with competitors' offerings, shifts in consumer needs, and so on.

Salespeople

Your own salespeople are good sources of marketing information. They more than anyone else come into direct contact with customers on a regular basis. This puts them in an ideal position to discover which customer needs are being overlooked and what new trends are developing as well as to detect changes in competitors' sales strategies. To make sure this information isn't wasted, you may find it useful to institute a reporting system that provides you with ready access to the findings of your salespeople.

Suppliers

Don't hesitate to ask your suppliers what's happening in the marketplace. A good supplier should do more than just fill your orders on time. Part of a supplier's job is to keep an eye on developments in his or her industry and to help business owners make the right purchasing decisions. This means knowing the details of a competitor's upcoming advertising campaign; the current research in your field; what new products are about to be launched; proposed price increases, and so on. Aside from the fact that a supplier may want you to place a large order, it's to the supplier's advantage to have you order only things appropriate for your business. After all, the continued success of each supplier depends on the success of the businesses he or she serves.

Trade Associations

Trade associations can provide you with marketing information in a variety of areas related to your business, including forecasts of future demand levels and trends; cost studies; statistics on your industry's policies, practices, and pay scales; the impact of proposed changes in government regulations, and so on. As a successful member of the business community, it's to your advantage to find out about trade associations that represent your industry.

Government

Government agencies at the federal, state, and local levels can supply you with a wealth of marketing research data at little or no cost. The Department of Commerce, Federal Trade Commission, Economic Development Offices, Internal Revenue Service, and the Small Business Administration are just a few of the agencies from which you can obtain information. In addition to having specialists on staff to answer specific questions, these agencies produce reports on all aspects of the economy, including population statistics (age, income, level of education, family status, and other demographic data), sales trends, building activity, housing units, and so on. Many of these reports are available at your local library. For an expanded list of what reports to look for, see "Government Reports and Periodicals" at the end of this chapter.

The Media

To spot the trends of tomorrow, it's important to be tuned into today. Successful business owners often become so involved in their business operations that they block out the outside world and fail to notice events that may affect their business. No matter how busy your schedule, each week set aside a certain percentage of your time to catch up on current events. By plugging into the media, you may find that an article in a newspaper or magazine or a program on radio or television can help to resolve a current problem or point your business in a new direction.

The Product Life Cycle

To anticipate changes in the demand for your products or services, or to evaluate the demand for new ones, you need to determine their positions within the product life cycle. Marketing researchers generally agree that all products and services evolve through a series of stages during which the demand for them peaks and eventually falls. As shown in the following chart, the product life cycle has four stages.

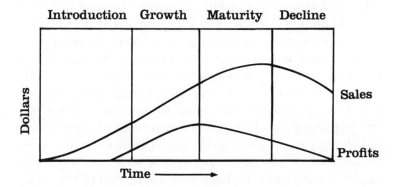

In the *introductory stage* the product isn't yet known to the general public. Whether the product has been newly invented (a solar-powered automobile) or is simply "new and improved" (a stronger soap detergent), it is seeking to become recognized. The marketing goal at this time is to educate potential customers about the benefits to be gained from using the product and to create an increasing demand for it.

In the *growth stage* a product is beginning to establish a name for itself. At this time both its sales volume and its profits should be growing at an accelerated rate as customers continue to discover and buy the product. Unfortunately, this same success soon attracts competitors. Unlike in the introductory stage, the question here isn't "What does the product do?" but "Which brand is best?"

In the *maturity stage* a product is well known by the public and may even be a leader in its field. However, given the heavy competition from similar products, its sales growth is already in the process of leveling off or even declining. In an effort to boost sales, promotion costs (advertising, cents-off coupons, special offers, and so on) are often increased during this stage. These have the desired effect of prolonging the product's life-span but also cut into its profits.

In the *decline stage* a product is nearing the end of its life cycle. Made obsolete by newer products, changes in customer preferences, or a saturated market, the product is no longer needed. At this stage profits may become virtually nonexistent as prices are slashed to increase the product's sales volume. But barring change in the product itself or in the market, this only serves to postpone the inevitable—replacing the old product with a more profitable one.

Although all products go through the product life cycle, the amount of time spent in any one stage, as well as the length of time from the beginning to the end of the cycle, varies for each product. A fad item, such as a new kitchen gadget, might have a life-span of less than a year, whereas a refrigerator today still has an indefinite life-span, at least until a better way of preserving food comes along. Savvy marketers have also discovered that by modifying a product or changing its image they can stretch the product life cycle, in effect creating a new and improved product. When this happens the product goes back to the beginning of the cycle and starts all over again. Thus, it's standard practice in many fields to avoid the decline stage, if at all possible, by continually updating the various products available.

Taking the workings of the product life cycle into consideration, you can determine whether a specific product needs to be promoted, modified, or discontinued. These considerations can also guide you in making the decision to add other products or services to those you already offer. The owner of a sporting goods store, for instance, may decide to increase the store's inventory of racquetball products because these are thought to be in the growth stage. At the same time, merchandise for another sport, which has moved into the maturity or decline stage, might be reduced or eliminated.

Generating New Ideas

Given the fact that even the best products and services can't stay in demand forever, the continued success of any business depends on its strength in developing new products. This process doesn't concern only manufacturing businesses, since a business's "product" may be a meal served in a restaurant, a haircut, or a selection of merchandise. Thus, one of your most important functions is to generate new ideas that result in successful products.

The more ideas you can generate for your business, the better chance you have of coming up with a money-making product. The Small Business Administration conducted a survey of major companies, each with millions of dollars to spend on marketing research and advertising and with a well-established distribution system, and found that of every fifty-eight ideas the companies generated, only twelve made it past the initial screening stage. And from those twelve ideas only one successful product emerged.

The SBA reported further that another group, which was set up to help businesses discover new ideas, found that of every hundred ideas submitted to it, eighty-five could be eliminated immediately as unworkable. As shown in the new-product development chart that follows, only fifteen ideas were felt to have any marketing potential. Of these, not more than five could be expected to be produced. And after all that, only one idea might eventually make money.

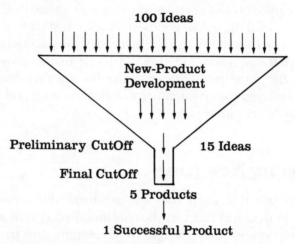

100 Ideas

New-Product Development

Preliminary CutOff   **15 Ideas**

Final CutOff

5 Products

1 Successful Product

NEW-PRODUCT DEVELOPMENT CHART

Considering the difficulty in conceiving just one profitable idea, you might find it surprising to discover that two sources of additional revenues—"throwaways" and "spinoffs"—may currently be going unnoticed in your business.

Throwaways

In your search for new profit opportunities, ask yourself, "Can any apparently useless by-products or throwaways be converted into money-makers?" The castoffs of many a business have turned into a gold mine for the person alert enough to recognize their profit potential. Damaged potatoes, though unsalable to grocery stores, can still be sold to food-processing companies for potato chips or instant mashed potato mixes. A wooden keg or shipping box in which your regular merchandise was delivered can be reused or even sold as a decorator item. Glass bottles and aluminum cans, instead of being discarded, should be recycled. Even used computer printouts can be salvaged and sold in bulk to recycling companies.

Spin-offs

Spin-offs—variations or extensions of your original products—can also provide additional revenues. In the fashion industry, for instance, the trend toward designer blue jeans has spun off jeans in other colors as well as the designer shirts, belts, and shoes to go with them. Consisting of new sizes, shapes, colors, flavors, styles, qualities, and so on, spin-offs eventually can become more profitable than the original products or services that launched them.

Recognizing the need for a safe, nondetergent shampoo, Marie Vega decided to create her own. "I wanted to do it with apple juice and honey and other good stuff," she says. So she got together with a chemist—who before going into the shampoo business used to do the hair of the Earl Carroll show girls—"and the two of us whipped it up." Originally the shampoo was intended for use only in Marie's salon, but as its popularity grew, she decided to distribute it through grocery stores, drugstores, and other outlets. To accomplish that she had to spin off a separate company, Marie Vega & Associates, Ltd., to manufacture and distribute the shampoo. Since then Marie has created a line of beauty products to go along with the shampoo, including a hair conditioner, face cream, and skin lotion.

Marie's products can now be found in stores throughout the United States. Customers can also order them directly from her company. Pointing to the public's greater awareness of health and nutrition, Marie expects the demand for her beauty products to rise. Differentiating them from other manufacturers' products, she says, "The important thing is what I *don't* put in. I don't put in thickeners, fillers, dyes, or detergents."

Whereas Marie Vega started with a salon and spun off a manufacturing and distribution company, Judy Cross started from the opposite direction. The owner of Tribal Arts, retail stores specializing in fine, southwestern Indian arts and crafts, she says, "The stores themselves are spin-offs." After running her own wholesaling business for several years, Judy started the stores to provide another market for her Indian art. "I supply all their inventory," she explains. "They are not allowed to buy anything from other suppliers except for things that I don't carry."

Within each store there are spin-offs, as well. In addition to high-quality jewelry and other Indian craft objects, the Tribal Arts stores carry books and greeting cards. This helps to increase the stores' overall sales volume by both adding to the dollar amount of individual sales and helping to turn browsers into buyers. Considering the number of tourists who come into her Virginia store, Judy says, "In Williamsburg I carry a few more touristy items, plastic dolls with feathers on top for kids. But not too many, and it's done as tastefully as one can do it. We also carry moccasins and hats." As to the value of spin-offs, Judy points out, "We sell a lot of moccasins to people who would never even consider buying Indian jewelry."

The Lettuce Patch restaurants were initially open only for lunch and dinner, but early-morning joggers, commuters, and others hungry for a light morning meal soon forced owners Elliot and Lois Schindel to spin off a breakfast menu. "People would come in and see us working in the morning," says Lois, "and they would say, 'Can I buy a cup of coffee?' I'd say, 'I'm sorry, we're not open yet.' Then they'd say, '*Please* sell me a cup of coffee. You don't even have to give me change. Here's fifty cents.' That's how it started." From then on things escalated, Lois recalls. "They started saying, 'Do you have any sweet rolls?' So we put in the croissants. Now we do a lot of fruit juice sales, and people will come in and ask, 'Do you have your fruit salad ready yet?' "

This willingness to respond to customers' needs extends to the rest of the bill of fare as well. In Lois' opinion, "You have to constantly change the menu and come up with new ideas." So, in addition to the do-it-yourself salads that The Lettuce Patch is known for, diners have a number of other food options to choose from, including homemade soups, sandwiches, quiche, and chili.

The success of their restaurants has led Elliot and Lois into an additional retail field. "We're distributing our own salad dressings," says Lois, delighted by the opportunity to reach still more people. "A whole retail operation has spun off of this." This means that those who have acquired a taste for Lois' unique salad dressings can also have them at home. Lois says that this development, like their other spin-offs, came about from a desire to meet their customers' needs: "The public directs what it wants."

Aside from the spin-offs in manufacturing and retail areas, more and more businesses are capitalizing on the opportunity to spin off their services. Barbara Koch, of Outstanding Stuff, says, "I also have an interior decorating service that spins off my business. It's actually a *re*decorating service. I go into peoples' homes and redesign their rooms with their own things. I very rarely remove anything. I just change it around." The same artist's sensibility that enables Barbara to find just the right things for her gift shop has proved an asset in her redecorating business. "I just have a knack for it," says Barbara. "I am very proficient at saving money. I know where to find things, how to buy things, the cheapest way to get around achieving the look that needs to be done for a certain room. Every time I do a house, I get one more house from it— their best friend, their sister, that kind of thing."

As word of Barbara's seemingly magical ability to transform an average house or apartment into a showplace continues to spread, it expands her client roster, which includes an increasing number of realtors eager to sell difficult listings. Builders and contractors are also turning to Barbara for help. Only instead of being asked to redo a house, it's to decorate the sales models!

New-Product Evaluation Table

To determine whether an idea for a new product or service has marketing potential, use the following new-product evaluation table to rate its suitability for your business. The more checks you put in the "excellent" or "good" columns, the greater the likelihood that the proposed product will be successful. Conversely, checks in the "fair" or "poor" columns represent product weaknesses that could limit your ability to develop and market the product successfully.

Product Characteristics	Excellent	Good	Fair	Poor
1. Compatibility with existing products or services	_____	_____	_____	_____
2. Compatibility with the business' image	_____	_____	_____	_____
3. Ability to be financed	_____	_____	_____	_____
4. Profit potential	_____	_____	_____	_____
5. Competitive strength	_____	_____	_____	_____
6. Life expectancy	_____	_____	_____	_____
7. Promotability	_____	_____	_____	_____
8. Patent protection	_____	_____	_____	_____
9. Compliance with legal requirements	_____	_____	_____	_____
10. Product safety	_____	_____	_____	_____

Government Reports and Periodicals

The following government reports and periodicals can help you stay informed in areas of economic development related to your business.

1. *Commerce Today.* U.S. Department of Commerce. Biweekly. Carries in its "International Commerce" section information and reports about various international markets, as well as news of specific sales opportunities. Sample copies may be obtained free from district offices.
2. *Construction Review.* U.S. Department of Commerce. GPO (Government Printing Office). Monthly. Brings together virtually all of the government's current statistics pertaining to construction, plus some nongovernmental statistical information.
3. *County and City Data Books.* Bureau of the Census, U.S. Department of Commerce. GPO. Presents statistical information on business, manufacturers, government, agriculture, population, housing, vital statistics, bank deposits, and other subjects. Issued every several years.
4. *County Business Patterns.* U.S. Department of Commerce. GPO. Annual. Separate book for each state and the District of Columbia; and one for Puerto Rico, American Samoa, Guam, and the U.S. Virgin Islands. Reports provide figures on first-quarter employment, taxable payroll data, number of reporting units, and number of units by employment size class for five hundred U.S. businesses and industries.
5. *Current Industrial Reports.* Bureau of the Census, U.S. Department of Commerce. These reports give information at the factory level for different industries on inventory, production, shipments, and other business activities.
6. *Current Business Reports.* Bureau of the Census, U.S.

Department of Commerce. GPO. Includes a series of four reports: *Weekly Retail Sales Report; Advance Monthly Retail Sales Report; Monthly Retail Trade;* and *Retail Annual Report.* Estimated retail-store sales by kinds of business, and some data for regions and metropolitan areas.

7. *Economic Indicators.* Prepared for the Joint Economic Committee by the Council of Economic Advisers. GPO. Monthly. Presents tables and charts dealing with prices, employment, wages, production and business activity, purchasing power, credit, and federal finance.

8. *Federal Reserve Bulletin.* Board of Governors of the Federal Reserve System. Monthly. Has monthly tables of financial and business statistics. Interest rates, money supply, consumer credit, and industrial production are some of the subjects included. Special articles cover the state of the economy, financial institutions, and statistical methodology.

9. *Monthly Labor Review.* U.S. Department of Labor. GPO. Monthly. The medium through which the Labor Department publishes its regular monthly reports on such subjects as trends of employment and payrolls, hourly and weekly earnings, working hours, collective agreements, industrial accidents, and disputes, as well as special features covering such topics as automation and profit sharing.

10. *Monthly Wholesale Trade Reports: Sales and Inventories.* Bureau of the Census, U.S. Department of Commerce. GPO. Reports trends in sales and inventories. Also gives some geographic data.

11. *Sources of State Information and State Industrial Directories.* Chamber of Commerce of the United States. Triennial. Contains names and addresses of private and public agencies that furnish information about their states. Also listed, under each state, are industrial directories and directories of manufacturers

published by state and private organizations. Some regional directories are included.

12. *State Bluebooks and Reference Publications.* Council of State Governments, Iron Works Pike, Lexington, Ky. A selected bibliography of bluebooks, reports, directories, and other reference publications produced by various departments of each state.

13. *Statistical Abstract of the United States.* Bureau of the Census, U.S. Department of Commerce. GPO. The standard summary of national statistics, it includes information on the labor force, population, business enterprise, and national income.

14. *Statistical Services of the United States Government.* Bureau of the Budget. GPO. Annual. Serves as a basic reference document on U.S. government statistical programs.

15. *Survey of Current Business.* U.S. Department of Commerce. GPO. Monthly. This periodical includes statistics and articles on significant economic developments. It presents statistics on national income, business population, manufacturers' sales, inventories, and orders, and carries special articles on personal income, foreign trade, and other aspects of the economy.

16. *U.S. Industrial Outlook.* U.S. Department of Commerce. GPO. Annual. Forecasts industry sales and employment for the following year and pinpoints industry trends. Analyses cover business prospects for 125 industries.

6 Time vs. Money

The Eternal Trade-off

ASIDE from the financial investment you've made in your business, you have to consider the investment of your time. Now that your business is operating smoothly, this might be the time to ease back a little or to work harder than ever. Each business owner must reassess how much time to devote to business. Often the question is, "Which is more important—additional leisure time or increased revenues?" Some business owners are discovering ways to have both.

Jim Mayhercy, partner with his wife, Daina, in 2nd Hand Tunes, a chain of used-record stores, says that in the future he "would like to spend about the same amount of time running the business, but would like to spend more 'quality' time." Jim has record stores throughout the Midwest and Florida and does most of the buying for the stores. In his search for used 45's, albums, and tapes, Jim says, "Some people bring in records to us, but I buy the majority on the road. I visit four to five homes every day and, since I started, I've been in every suburb and neighborhood of Chicago."

Jim's hectic schedule is dictated to a great extent by the record-buying public's seemingly insatiable demand for out-of-circulation and classic records, or just for a bargain. He says, "Our clients are mostly adults who are looking for the variety in records you can't find these days. Records go out of print quickly, and record stores carry mostly the giant hits. We carry everything, and at a third to a half of what you pay elsewhere." But stocking his record bins and racks with the right records is time-consuming and requires Jim's personal attention. Explains Jim, "I must determine if the current hits will stand the test of time, or whether records that seem obscure now will be of great interest in the future." Maintaining 2nd Hand Tunes' inventory level calls for Jim to have the instincts and nerve of a commodities broker. What's more, given the increased competition, as others enter the used-record field, it's getting tougher to find the records he wants. Somehow Jim manages to keep everything in perspective. He limits his work to "no more than forty hours a week" and—something almost unheard-of among many entrepreneurs—still finds time to take vacations.

Time—An Accountable Asset

Time, like any other asset used in your business, should be allocated wisely. Yet the same business owners who can account for each dollar spent on behalf of their businesses often find themselves at a loss when it comes to itemizing their expenditures of time. When pressed to keep a log of their daily activities, they find that the percentage of time occupied by business concerns is sometimes staggering— not just nine-to-five time, but also time spent planning, thinking, communicating, traveling, and so on. Even those businesspersons who claim to "leave the business at the office" may be startled to see how many hours they actually spend running their businesses.

Hourly workers know to the minute how much time they spend on the job. But business owners may be working the equivalent of an extra day or more without even realizing it. This is not to say that it's wrong to spend so much time, or that the owner should cut back on the hours spent on the job, but that business owners should *know* where their time goes. As Jim Mayhercy points out, more important than the quantity of time you put into your business is the quality of that time.

Increasing Your Quality Time

Quality time—when you are actively pursuing your goals creatively and constructively—can be hard to come by. To maximize the amount of quality time available for business issues, you must first overcome certain obstacles. These include a variety of "time wasters" which, when totaled, can actually eclipse the amount of time spent productively. As shown here, some of these time wasters are unavoidable, but, through proper planning, most can be reduced or even eliminated.

Time wasters:

• Telephone interruptions
• Unscheduled appointments
• Inadequate filing system
• Unorganized desk
• Lack of information
• Key personnel unavailable
• Needless paperwork
• Failure to delegate
• Procrastination
• Lack of priorities
• Personnel problems
• Duplicated efforts
• Misunderstandings
• Insufficient planning
• Indecision

- Commuting
- Insufficient office layout
- Spreading yourself too thin
- Not saying no
- Fatigue

The secret to getting past these obstacles is to implement a time management system and *use* it. Far from being complex, a system as simple as the one that follows may save you considerable amounts of time and money by increasing your productivity.

An Entrepreneur's Time Management System

Set priorities. Determine in advance what goals you wish to accomplish, on both a short-term and a long-term basis, and rank them in order of importance. Then focus on those items that have the highest priority. Items with low priorities should be delegated to someone else, postponed, or eliminated.

Delegate. One of the hardest tasks for many business owners is delegating. Rather than assigning part of the work load to competent employees, they try to do everything themselves. Rationalizing this reluctance to delegate on the basis of being "the only one qualified to do the work," the owner is afraid to relinquish control to others. This strategy results not only in poor utilization of employee talents, but of the owner's talents as well. As a rule of thumb, all tasks should be delegated to the lowest level of competence in the organization.

Identify high-productivity hours. In allocating your time it helps to identify those hours during the day when you are at peak efficiency. Some people work better in the morning, but others don't reach their stride until afternoon. You may find that you have periods of peak efficiency scattered throughout the day. Whatever your pattern, you should identify these times and reserve them, whenever possible, for those high-priority items on your list of things to do. Items with a lower priority can be accomplished during the times when you are usually less productive.

Set aside quiet time. A time-management technique used by many successful business owners is to designate a specific period during the day as "quiet time." Ranging from forty-five minutes to two hours, this is a period you can use to think, plan, reflect, read, and so on. During this time no meetings are scheduled, and only those phone calls requiring immediate attention are accepted. Some owners have found this technique so helpful in increasing their own productivity that they've asked their management personnel to adopt it too.

Outline procedures in advance. One way to reduce interruptions and to get needed information more easily is to outline procedures in advance. This makes clear to others not only how they can gain access to you, but also how you wish to have access to them. Rather than having to attend personally to each situation or wait for vital information, the system handles it for you.

Plan meetings and phone calls. Meetings and phone calls are essential to doing business. Yet as most business owners agree, they can also be some of the least productive parts unless they are planned in advance. When making a business phone call, decide what you want to say before placing the call. Then say it as clearly and concisely as possible. Before scheduling a meeting, ask yourself exactly what the meeting is to accomplish. Then plan the agenda accordingly, eliminating irrelevant topics. Don't forget to make sure that employees whose information is needed will attend.

Cut back on needless paperwork. As businesses increase in size, so does the amount of paperwork. If not checked, the level of paperwork can become more important than the products or services the business creates. To avoid this, needless paperwork should be cut back whenever possible. For instance, a phone call often suffices in place of a letter.

And rather than writing up a routine report or evaluation, perhaps you can fill out a form.

Coordinate activities. To avoid duplicated efforts, it helps to coordinate your business activities so you have all the information and materials you need to tackle the problem at hand. Rather than working on a piecemeal basis or trying to go in two directions at once, you can link all activities together.

Communicate clearly. Misunderstandings and costly mistakes can frequently be avoided by taking the time to communicate clearly. Though it may take a little longer to compose your thoughts and determine precisely what you want to say or write, in the long run you'll save time. That time, which might otherwise be spent reclarifying your objective or waiting for a mistake to be corrected, will be available for new activities.

Use remnant time. Remnant time—the intervals between scheduled activities—is quite often wasted. Fifteen minutes here, twenty-five minutes there. By itself they aren't much, but by the end of the day, they all add up. One way to have more quality time for high-priority items is to use these odd remnants of time to take care of low-priority or routine items, such as returning a phone call, catching up on your reading, and so on.

To implement the preceding time-management system, you might find it helps to use a daily planner similar to the one in the following chart. Unlike a conventional calendar, this chart enables you to assign priorities to your activities and assists you in delegating activities that can be performed by others.

Your Own Priorities

In setting the priorities for your business, set your personal priorities too. What do you hope to achieve through

DAILY PLANNER

Date _____			Schedule
Things to Do			**A.M.**
_____		_____	
			7:00
_____		_____	
			8:00
_____		_____	
			9:00
_____		_____	
			10:00
_____		_____	
			11:00
_____		_____	
			P.M.
Priorities	**✓ Completed Comments**	**Name of Person Delegated to**	12:00
Top			1:00
			2:00
High			3:00
			4:00
Med.			5:00
Low			**Evening**

the business? What do you want from the business? How much time are you willing to put into it?

Asked how much time she invests in her business, Karen York responds quickly, "Whatever it takes!" Barbara Alpern, Karen's partner in the York Group, agrees with her totally. "We did not start this business, nor would Karen and I be partners, if either one of us said, 'I'm only going to spend thirty hours a week, and I need two hours for lunch, and on Wednesdays I go to my shrink, and I have a hair appointment at one o'clock on Fridays!' If either one of us thought like that, it would not make for a good union. We work evenings. We work weekends. We meet for breakfast to discuss the issues. We work through lunch. We're working all the time."

Virtually living and breathing their work at all times, Karen says, "We both have tape recorders in our cars to pick up ideas, and pens and pencils next to our beds." Driven by sheer enthusiasm and the will to succeed, Karen admits to being the type of businessperson who needs to be forced to take a vacation. And on more than one occasion, that's actually happened. "I sometimes call her in," says Barbara, "and tell her, 'You're getting very testy. You're making things tense around here. What are you doing to take care of yourself?' " "She sent me away for the weekend," says Karen with a laugh. "She let me know that if I didn't take time for myself, I was in big trouble."

"At this stage in the business, I don't know if I'm working harder or not," says Fred Salenger. "When you're starting out, in some ways it takes a great deal more time to get all the systems down." In any event, he points out, "The problems change. The jobs have changed." His educational products company, Salenger Educational Media, does more now, but it also has more people and a sophisticated computer system to take care of the work load.

As for his future plans, Fred emphasizes, "I'm *not* a

workaholic and I'm not going to kill myself over profits." However, he makes it clear that "each business is different. If I were in a high-technology industry with extreme competition on my back, like it or not, I might be forced to work harder. This is a more laid-back business because of the nature of the creativity. We don't have any real competition . . . because the product is so different. Either they like it or they don't. With a [management training or motivation] film, if it meets the corporation's needs, it works, and they buy it." Noting this lack of competitive pressure, Fred observes, "Maybe that's why I'm not a workaholic. Because the industry doesn't demand it." Thus, having managed to avoid making a trade-off between increased leisure and additional revenues, he asks optimistically, "Why can't I have both?"

Judy Cross of Tribal Arts raises the point that for many entrepreneurs, work isn't so much an option as a way of life. "I say I'd like to cut back. But I'm not sure what I'd do with my time if I didn't work. I pretend that I'd love to take a vacation, but if I went to the islands or something like that, I'd be so antsy I'd want to get back. So I want to learn how to relax a bit. I really don't know how to."

On those rare occasions when she has time to relax, Judy tends to end up doing something business-related, even if it's just "shuffling papers." As she describes it, "The time is always spent with something about the business in my head. It's never spent playing tennis, which I don't do, or sunning." Her one recreation of sorts is traveling. "It's fun getting on a plane," she says. "I look forward to it."

Frequently on the road for one to three weeks at a time, Judy is always on the lookout for the high-quality Indian crafts and jewelry that she can sell in her stores. Although there are moments when spending so much time away from home admittedly bothers her, she says, "I don't think I could ever go back to the nine-to-five life-style. I do enjoy my business."

Family Considerations

What about your family? Where do they fit into the business plan? When you chart the direction your business will follow, it's important that you consider the needs of individual family members too.

For Doug Stephen of Modern Fasteners, Inc., this didn't always come easily. "I had a lot of maturing and a lot of growing up to do," he says. "During the sixties, when my children were born, I was taught, like a lot of people, that work came first, family came second. It took me a long time to put things in perspective, that really your family is first."

Now when he's in an important meeting, Doug says, "I refuse to take all phone calls . . . with the exception of my family's." This wasn't always the case: "There was a time where I would say, 'I'm sorry, Barbara, I can't talk to you. I'm in conference.' " Not anymore. In addition to making himself much more accessible to his family, Doug also has become involved in his children's schools, serving in such capacities as president of the parents' association at one school and as a member of the board of regents at another. This, he says, not only enables him to use his organizational skills but also to fulfill his responsibility as a parent.

In keeping with this desire to bridge the gap between his personal and his business priorities, Doug has also reduced his daily commuting time. In its current location Modern Fasteners is only five minutes from his home. Now, rather than having to choose whether to work late at the office or have dinner with his family, Doug can do both. "Many times, if something has to be done," he says, "I'll come back down to the office after dinner to do it."

After carving out a name for himself on the East Coast in the supermarket field, Herb Reiner made some radical changes. Uprooting his family, he moved to Southern

California and started his new business, Vitamin City. And in addition to these changes, he also changed his priorities about work and family. Like Doug Stephen, Herb began making a concerted effort to spend more time with his family.

Pleased by the "new" Herb, his wife, Binnie, says, "Michael, our oldest son, never used to see Herb. Many times Herb would leave before Michael got up in the morning and by the time he came home at night Michael was sleeping. It was horrible." The grocery business was so demanding that Binnie rarely got a chance to see Herb either. What's more, when she did see him, he was exhausted, or, in Herb's words, "like a zombie."

That's all changed. Living just a mile from his office and with a flexible time schedule, Herb is healthier and happier than ever before. Now, if he wants to stay home on a weekend, he does. "There isn't this driving force pulling him into the store anymore," says Binnie, adding that, compared to Michael, their youngest son, Barry, "is seeing a lot more of his father." As for her own reaction to having her husband returned to her again, Binnie exclaims, "It's like being newlyweds after twenty-five years!"

7 Pulling the Strings

Who's in Charge?

ONE of the major decision areas confronting each business owner is the matter of authority. How much authority should be delegated? To whom? The way you answer these questions will, to a great extent, determine not only the organizational structure of your business but also its level of accomplishment.

Richard LaMotta, of Chipwich, Inc., believes in delegating liberal amounts of authority to employees at all levels in his company, from top to bottom. Actively seeking out and hiring problem solvers, he says, "When I give a job to a person, I don't want him to come to me and say; 'I can't do this. I've got a problem.' There are no problems. There are ways around every problem. Find the crack. . . . Solve the problem." In addition to expecting employees to use their own initiative, he also provides them with ample opportunities to be creative. "Everybody can be creative. I encourage that," emphasizes Richard. "I say, 'Be creative. I may not take your idea as it comes in. Maybe I'll modify it and put our little flair on it—the LaMotta instinct for Chipwich—but I won't take your idea and not give credit for it. And, if you come up with something, there'll be a reward in it for you. So be creative.' "

"I'd rather have 10 percent of something big than 90 percent of nothing" is Richard's policy, so he has employees share in both the responsibilities and the rewards associated with the success of Chipwich, Inc. He makes just one exception to this: "The one area that I don't think can be delegated is that of spokesman—the public relations and advertising, the public image of the company and the promotion. Chipwich is the product of a personality, and that personality is myself. Let's face it, you don't let go of that. You don't want someone else out telling your story."

What Can Be Delegated?

Depending on the nature of each business' products or services, certain areas of operation may require greater degrees of owner control than others. As shown in the table on the following page such areas cover the spectrum of business activities.

Place a check mark in the appropriate box opposite each control category, thereby indicating whether a low, medium, or high degree of control is required.

In areas of your business requiring a high degree of control, most of the authority is likely to be retained by you. Conversely, in areas needing a low degree of control, most of the authority is likely to be delegated to others.

Asked to pinpoint the area of her business that requires the highest degree of control, Lina Lidow says, "Buying is the most important. I do all of the buying for all of the Lina Lee stores right now." No easy feat, this entails choosing from among the fashion collections of eighty-five different designers every season, as well as scouting those up-and-coming designers who have yet to be discovered. Lina is reluctant to delegate in this area because in the fashion industry buying is a highly subjective activity, depending almost totally on the visual perceptions of the

DEGREE OF OWNER CONTROL REQUIRED

Control area	Low	Med.	High
Finances	_____	_____	_____
Production	_____	_____	_____
Quality control	_____	_____	_____
Customer service	_____	_____	_____
Distribution	_____	_____	_____
Sales	_____	_____	_____
Advertising	_____	_____	_____
Purchasing	_____	_____	_____
Personnel	_____	_____	_____
Inventory control	_____	_____	_____
Promotion	_____	_____	_____
Research and development	_____	_____	_____

buyer. Lina says, "When I see the color red, I see it one way. Someone else sees it a different way." This discrepancy, she explains, limits her ability to send out a buyer then "call and say, 'Quick, buy any shirts you can find that are that beautiful Chinese red color.' Well, what is Chinese red? It becomes very difficult."

Lina's eye for color, not to mention for fabric and style, has been a major factor in the success of each Lina Lee boutique. "One reason we've been able to do the volume we do is because everything is coordinated," she observes. "The reds match. The blues match. If I say royal blue, it's royal blue . . . based on my eyes." Often this can mean the difference between making a sale and not making a sale, Lina points out. If a customer is buying a red suit by one designer "but hates that designer's red shirt, we can pull seven different designers' shirts to match that red."

To stay on top of things, especially since opening boutiques in New York City's Trump Tower, Lina makes extensive use of telexes. These are extremely helpful, she notes, "because they are usually a quick summary of what's going on with a specific designer. A telex doesn't cover everything, but it covers certainly any problems or anything pressing for that particular moment."

Franchisor Lois Schindel, of The Lettuce Patch self-service salad bar restaurant, admits, "I tend not to let people take control altogether. I do not like to let go." Most concerned about quality control, she says, "If I had to watch for one thing only, it would be the freshness and the appearance of our salad bar. This is one area I am absolutely insane about." Elliot Schindel, on the other hand, says that his area is "strictly design. We planned this thing so that I would design the restaurants, build them and put in the equipment, and Lois would operate them." Dividing the responsibility this way enables Elliot and Lois to capitalize on their individual talents while virtually eliminating points of conflict. "Although we're in the same business," notes Elliot, "she has her space and I have mine. And together we have our space. I will not interfere in Lois' space unless she asks and," he says, laughing, "she will not interfere in what I'm doing because she doesn't *know* what I'm doing. She can't read blueprints, and I can."

Despite the fact that they are in constant communication with each other twenty-four hours a day, Lois says, "We still look forward to being alone together." "The amazing part about all this," remarks Elliot, "is that we get along so well together. I have heard so many stories where husbands and wives work in the same area and inevitably they end up arguing and getting divorces. This is just so unbelievable to me."

Summing up in one word the area of his business that requires the greatest degree of control, Doug McDonald says, "money." To keep Planning Counselors, Incorporated on target, he oversees everything pertaining to finances. "Right now I am handling all the financial aspects for a couple of reasons," Doug explains. "Number one, we need a lot of control in that area. Number two, I enjoy it." Aside from just watching the budget and trying to reduce expenses whenever possible, Doug spends a great deal of his time forecasting, analyzing the company's current cash position, and projecting its future needs. He recommends that business owners who have no background in finance take a course or seminar on the subject. "Watching the expenses is one thing," he points out, "but you also have to watch the cash flow." For his part, Doug tries "to see how the money is flowing, to anticipate what the impact of the economy is going to be on our accounts receivable and what that will cause to happen."

The Delegation Process

A frequent mistake by business owners and managers is to assume that by delegating authority to a subordinate, the delegation process is complete. In fact, authority is just one of three elements in the delegation process. The other two—responsibility and accountability—must also be present if you are to get positive results.

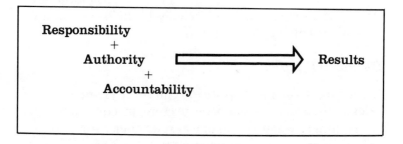

Responsibility

The delegation process starts with assigning specific responsibilities. What the employee is expected to do should be fully explained at the time he or she is hired, promoted, transferred, or given a new assignment. Referring to all the job functions or activities necessary to fulfill an assignment, responsibility should generally be delegated to the lowest level of competence in your business.

Authority

In delegating authority to an employee, you are giving him or her the right to make decisions and the power to carry them out. The amount of authority that should be delegated depends on the nature of each employee's job assignment and responsibilities. At a minimum, delegate enough authority (1) to get the work done, (2) to allow key employees to take initiative, and (3) to keep things going in your absence.

Accountability

Accountability refers to the obligation all employees have to fulfill the responsibilities that have been assigned to them. However, unlike the other two elements in the delegation process, accountability cannot be delegated. It is something that an employee chooses to accept or not to accept. If an employee rejects his or her obligation, then you, as the owner, must ultimately be held accountable. This should always be kept in mind.

The Parity Principle

According to the parity principle, all three elements of the delegation process should be present in equal amounts. For example, when you assign responsibility for a specific task to an employee, the activities to be performed should not exceed the employee's authority to carry them out. Thus, if you give your secretary a major project to complete, such as preparing a slide show for an upcoming meeting, the secretary must also have the authority to obtain the necessary information to be included in the presentation.

The amount of authority delegated should be in proportion to each employee's responsibilities. The employee who has more authority than responsibility often feels underutilized and unappreciated. ("I could do more if they'd give me a chance.") On the other hand, the employee who has too little authority tends to feel helpless and ineffectual. ("Don't bother me. I can't cope.")

As for accountability, proper screening and training of employees, along with proper delegation, can help to bring this in balance with the other two elements. However, employees should not be expected to accept an obligation that exceeds their areas of responsibility or authority. After all, without the skills or power to do the job, it would be unfair to hold them accountable for it.

Centralized vs. Decentralized Authority

The amount of authority you delegate and how extensively it is spread throughout your business determine whether the business' organizational structure is centralized or decentralized. If little or no authority is delegated, a business is centralized. In this case, the owner alone, or perhaps with a small group of top managers, makes most of the decisions concerning the business. If, however, authority is widely distributed among employees at all levels in the business, it is decentralized. In this case, employees participate in most of the decision-making.

To determine which of these two approaches to delegation best suits the current needs of your business, first compare the advantages and disadvantages of each. These are shown in the table on page 105.

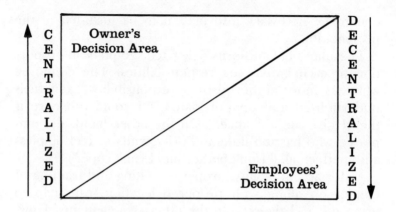

DISTRIBUTION OF AUTHORITY

There is something to be said for both approaches to delegation. It isn't so much a question of determining which is better, but rather which is better for *you*. In practice you may find that a combination of the two suits your situation best.

In assessing the degree of decentralization that would be beneficial for your business, you might also find it helpful to consider these factors:

- The costs involved
- The impact on your business' policies and practices
- The skills and talents of your employees
- The willingness of employees to accept accountability
- Employees' access to information
- The speed in which decisions must be made
- The effect on employee morale
- Your own willingness to relinquish control

"Right now I probably need less control than I exert," says Doug McDonald of Planning Counselors, Incorporated. "But it's a matter of training people up. A big breakthrough for us was putting somebody in a purely administrative position. Always before, everybody had a job and a

CENTRALIZED AUTHORITY

Advantages	Disadvantages
You can make quick decisions.	You may not have enough information to make a decision.
Decisions conform to the same standards.	Greater demands are placed on you and your top managers.
Policies can be uniformly implemented.	Decisions often reflect a narrow viewpoint.
Accountability can be readily determined.	You receive less feedback from employees.
The level of duplicated effort is reduced.	Employees at lower levels may feel left out.
Less time is spent in meetings.	
Activities can be coordinated more easily.	

DECENTRALIZED AUTHORITY

Advantages	Disadvantages
You can spend more time focusing on key areas.	More time is spent getting a consensus of opinion.
Employees can deal with problems as they occur.	A greater amount of time and money is spent on training.
Employees gain experience in decision-making.	The consistency and quality of decisions may vary.
Employees are more likely to be strongly motivated.	It can undermine the unity of the business' objectives.
It's easier to expand your business.	Accountability is harder to establish.
The skills and abilities of all employees can be utilized.	

chunk of the administration too. But you get to the point where you say, 'Wait a minute. We need somebody who is *not* producing but is administering.' "

Prior to this move, Doug was so involved in day-to-day decisions that he could scarcely find time for long-range planning and other top-priority items. Furthermore, although the employees all shared in the decision-making process, since it was on a piecemeal basis, it involved a great amount of duplicated effort. And their added responsibility, instead of improving morale, was actually lowering it. The answer to Doug's problem and that of his employees was to use a combination approach to delegation. In effect, he chose a form of limited decentralization. Creating the administrative position removed part of the responsibility not only from Doug but also from PCI's employees, freeing Doug from many of the day-to-day activities and enabling employees to perform their assignments better. Morale improved, and so did productivity.

Commenting on this new arrangement, Doug says, "I work closely with that person in the administrative position and have found a lot that he can do for me." However, Doug cautions, "A lot of times people delegate only the crummy jobs, not the good ones. You have to give some of the peaches too."

Sue Jones-Allen of the interior design and contracting firm Up Against the Wall has found that decentralization enables her to establish areas of profit responsibility. She explains, "Because each supervisor is very autonomous, they rise and fall in direct proportion to their own input." This is much the same principle used by major manufacturers in setting up divisions, then holding the division managers accountable for the profitable operation of their units.

Elaborating on this approach, Sue states, "There are *no* hourly employees [at Up Against the Wall]. They are all responsible for all equipment, tools, etc. They even collect the money." Working as a team, Sue and each supervisor determine the price of a job before it is bid out. Then, once the work has been completed, Sue checks to make sure it has been performed properly. Here, she notes, "if a job is botched, we share the cost of rectifying the error, if it is an honest mistake. Otherwise they don't get paid."

Describing herself as "very noncritical but definite about my standards," Sue emphasizes that "there is no flexibility here." After experimenting with a more centralized system of delegation, both she and her staff are pleased with the results of this approach. In Sue's words, "They feel very much in charge but always know I have the final power."

Span of Control

A separate area of delegation, which goes hand in hand with centralization and decentralization, is span of control. A basic part of the organizational structure of your business, this refers to the number of workers who report to each supervisor. If your business is small, it's likely that each worker reports directly to you. If this is the case, your span of control is equal to the number of employees who work for you.

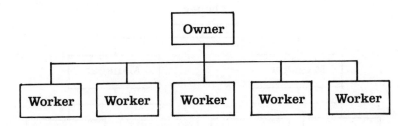

If your business expands, span of control becomes more important. At this stage you must decide what is the ideal number of workers you can supervise. Furthermore, with the addition of each manager to aid in the supervision process, his or her span of control must be determined. As shown in the following chart, narrowing your span of control and that of your managers increases the organizational levels needed.

Wide Span of Control (4 persons)
4 Managers
2 Levels of Management

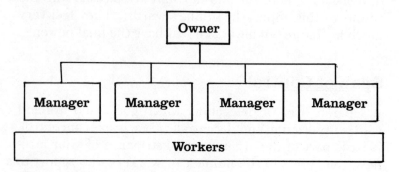

Narrow Span of Control (2 persons)
6 Managers
3 Levels of Management

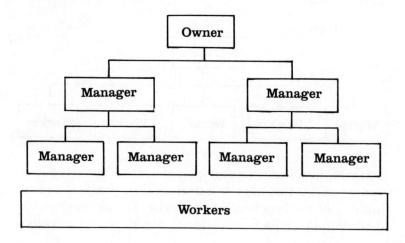

Ultimately it comes down to a choice between a wide span of control and a few levels (or even one level) of management, or a narrow span of control and more levels of management. The wide span gives you and your managers greater control, but it also puts a greater burden of responsibility on you. The narrow span relieves this burden but, by adding extra levels, it is more costly and makes communication more complicated.

Although on the surface it might seem like a simple matter of mathematics, determining the appropriate span of control is more involved than that. In fact, no one span of control works best. Each situation and each person is different. One manager may be perfectly at ease supervising twenty or more employees, but another manager is uncomfortable with three. In evaluating your current situation or anticipating future needs, keep in mind:

1. *Your own skills as a manager.* Many entrepreneurs are excellent at coming up with new ideas but have difficulty implementing them. This may be due to lack of management training, lack of time, or both. Narrowing the span of control can compensate for this.

2. *The skills of your current managers or those in line for management positions.* The greater their abilities, the wider the span of control that can be used.

3. *The competence of the employees being supervised.* When employees can be counted on to work competently and independently, there can be a wider span of control.

4. *The activities being performed.* Activities that are basically similar and routine usually can be handled with a wide span of control. Conversely, dissimilar activities normally require a narrow span of control.

5. *The size of your business.* Generally as a business grows—whether in number of employees or locations, or product lines—the span of control gets narrower.

This is particularly true at the owner's level, since it enables the owner to focus on fewer decision areas at a time.

6. *The presence of set policies and procedures.* The extent to which policies and procedures are set in advance also affects the span of control. The more they are predetermined, the wider the span of control possible.

In keeping with their desire to be personally involved in all aspects of their business on both a day-to-day and a long-range basis, Annie and Biddy Hurlbut have opted for a wide span of control. As Annie explains, "Each employee [at The Peruvian Connection] has a realm of responsibility but is involved in and occasionally participates in all others." In this way, she adds, "We don't have any middle managers to compromise direct communication between owners and employees." However, Annie points out that given the continued success of her catalogue business, "maybe this system would have to change with growth."

For the moment, anyway, span of control isn't a problem. Vowing to have "more products but never mass production," Annie plans to keep The Peruvian Connection relatively small, in one location. "We see growth by a factor of ten rather than a hundred times present level."

Whatever systems of control you currently use—centralized authority or decentralized authority, a wide or narrow span of control—there's a good chance you will have to modify them. In what appears to be a growing trend, more and more successful businesses are recognizing the need to develop flexible organization structures. Rather than selecting what seems to be the perfect system of control and then sticking with it no matter what, businesses are striving to adapt to change.

8 Business and Pleasure

Why Not Have Fun?

DURING the pivotal phase of your business' development, don't lose sight of one of the fundamental reasons for going into business in the first place—to have fun. Successful entrepreneurs know not only how to run their businesses but also how to enjoy their success.

Alice Byrne, of Ambassador Special Services, Ltd., states emphatically that running her private investigation agency is "quite simply fun." To keep it this way she strives to maintain an environment in which she is "not overextended, yet challenged significantly." Formerly a registered nurse, Alice is well aware of the physical and mental dangers of trying to do too much too fast or becoming totally consumed by one's business. As a result, she says, "I carefully plan my leisure time with my family, delegate responsibilities and set slow growth goals."

These precautions and the fact that Alice enjoys her work notwithstanding, she admits that stress and the potential for stress are still very real concerns. "Each success brings its share of responsibility," notes Alice. "As jobs are added, they must be maintained." Along with this, she has come to realize that "failure is no longer a personal experience but will affect others' careers." Given this increased level of responsibility, "dealing with the stress success brings has been a drain on inner resources," says Alice. She feels that she has been required to draw as much on her personal resiliency as on her skills as an entrepreneur.

Dealing with Stress

One of the greatest threats to your enjoyment of your business and your well-being as an entrepreneur may come not from without but within. Overshadowing such uncontrollable dangers as aggressive competitors, changes in the economy, and shifting markets, it is a danger that you alone can control: your own reaction to stress.

To deal with stress, it helps to know exactly what it is and how it affects you. Stress itself is any threat—real or imagined—to your personal well-being. In the context of your business activities, stress could result from almost anything—from your fear of losing your market share to a competitor, to impatience over having a long-distance telephone call put on hold. More important than the nature of the stress, however, are your reactions to it. These can range from being irritable and perspiring to such major problems as high blood pressure and ulcers.

As shown in the table that follows, the presence of certain warning signals is often a sign of stress. The fact that you may agree with some of these statements doesn't by itself mean you are experiencing stress. However, it is a possibility that should be explored. This calls for you to do two things: learn how to identify stress and develop ways to control it.

Identifying Stress

The first step in dealing with stress is to identify it. Once you are able to recognize which business activities or situations are stressful for you, you will be better equipped to take corrective action to bring them under control. This

WARNING SIGNALS OF STRESS

	Agree	Disagree
1. I feel tired most of the time.	_____	_____
2. I frequently have headaches.	_____	_____
3. My stomach is often upset.	_____	_____
4. I have high blood pressure.	_____	_____
5. I feel I should be accomplishing more.	_____	_____
6. I procrastinate too much.	_____	_____
7. Little things make me irritable.	_____	_____
8. I expect a lot from myself.	_____	_____
9. I don't like criticism.	_____	_____
10. It's hard to keep track of appointments.	_____	_____
11. Sometimes my mind wanders.	_____	_____
12. There are always more decisions to be made.	_____	_____
13. I'd like to slow down but can't.	_____	_____
14. I don't feel comfortable delegating to others.	_____	_____
15. My objectives keep changing.	_____	_____
16. The business always demands more from me.	_____	_____
17. The competition is usually on my mind.	_____	_____
18. Half the time customers don't know what they want.	_____	_____
19. The market changes so fast, it's hard to keep up.	_____	_____
20. I don't have enough time to spend with my family.	_____	_____

may call for eliminating or reducing the source of stress or, if this is not feasible, learning positive ways to adapt to it.

Television producers Bob Conlin and Mary Mangan, a husband-and-wife team and the co-owners of Tape, Inc., find that working together helps to alleviate stress by enabling them to share their business responsibilities. Still, when stress occurs, they know how debilitating it can be. Recalling one stressful experience in particular, Bob says, "We did one project that I worked on so hard, I would get sick every day." Unable to pinpoint the reason for this at the time, he finally figured out that it was because he didn't enjoy the project. "Instead of producing a television program, it was a slide presentation," Bob explains. "They paid a lot of money, but we really didn't like doing it."

Having learned from this experience, Bob and Mary now try to limit their projects, whenever possible, to those that are meaningful for them. "One of our hopes and dreams," says Mary, "is to be able to turn down anything that doesn't give us pleasure." A project that obviously gives them pleasure is a series of television programs called *Coasting*. The series focuses on country inns throughout the United States, enabling Bob and Mary to combine their love of travel with that of television production.

Bob Conlin reduces the level of business-related stress by choosing television projects he really believes in. Marie Vega, on the other hand, discovered that she needed to cut back on the number of hours she was putting into her hair salon and beauty products business. Like many entrepreneurs, she had become so wrapped up in her business, Marie Vega & Associates, that she had virtually *become* the business. "To put the fun back in, I've had to separate the business from my personal life," says Marie. "Now, as much as I want to stay, when it's five-thirty, I say, 'I'm leaving the mess and I'm going to go.' I just have to do it, that tearing away. Because I wasn't putting in good quality time anymore."

Working fewer hours has benefited Marie and her business as well. Distancing herself from the business gives her a new perspective, she explains. "I notice that now, if I get away from it and I lay back and relax, my mind starts working, ideas start coming in, I get freed." Comparing her approach to work and her feelings about good nutrition, Marie points out that balance is important in both. "Just as you're not going to eat chicken or anything else all the time, I don't have to do the same thing all the time. I can mix it up and make a good combination. If I don't, no matter how many things I'm doing right, the stress is going to kill me."

When it comes to running your business, the more in tune you are with your own preferences, the greater your ability to keep stress to a minimum. It's not uncommon for entrepreneurs to realize suddenly that the business activities they enjoy most are the ones they do least, and vice versa. This can be due to a shift in responsibilities, a change in the direction of the business, or to any number of other reasons. Whatever the cause, a disparity between what you like to do and what you actually do can easily take the pleasure out of your business.

To determine how closely the business activities you prefer to do match those you actually do, take a moment to answer the entrepreneur's preference test.

ENTREPRENEUR'S PREFERENCE TEST

In the first column rank those activities you prefer to do, putting the numeral "1" by your favorite activity, and so on. In the second column rank those activities you actually do, putting the numeral "1" by the activity you spend the most time doing, and so on.

Business Activities	Prefer to Do	Actually Do
Administering	_____	_____
Representing the business	_____	_____
Creating	_____	_____
Performing technical duties	_____	_____
Thinking	_____	_____
Communicating	_____	_____
Interacting with others	_____	_____
Planning	_____	_____
Buying	_____	_____
Selling	_____	_____
Training employees	_____	_____
Motivating	_____	_____
Researching	_____	_____
Forecasting	_____	_____

How did they match up? Ideally, you should spend more time on those activities you prefer and less time on the others. If not, what can you do to improve the situation? Changing your priorities, delegating more, reorganizing the business, hiring additional personnel, or using outside consultants are possible solutions from which to choose.

Ways to Control Stress

Although it is impossible to eliminate all stress from your life, you can employ various strategies to minimize its effect. The following suggestions should help you gain control over stress directly related to your business.

1. *Avoid being a perfectionist.* Trying to do your best and encouraging others to do the same is one thing, but setting unreasonable standards of perfection is another. Recognize that it is not always possible to operate at a 100-percent efficiency level. Make allowances when necessary. After all, you're only human.

2. *Savor your accomplishments.* Rather than rushing from one activity to the next, take time to enjoy the moment at hand—successfully completing a project, satisfying a customer, solving a problem, and so on. You might just find that these moments are the best things of all about being in business.

3. *Remain flexible.* One of the greatest causes of stress is nothing more than change itself, or, more accurately, the unwillingness of individuals to accept it—even when the change could be for the better. By keeping your options open, you can minimize your reaction to change-induced stress and possibly capitalize on new opportunities.

4. *Develop a support network.* No matter how busy you are, it's important to make time to build and maintain friendships with others both within your industry and outside it. This not only helps to increase your level of self-esteem and provide reassurance that others want you to succeed, but also can be a valuable source of information. Long known to be an essential aid for managers, networking is just as necessary, if not more so, for business owners.

5. *Watch your diet.* Despite the temptation to skip meals or eat foods high in fats, sugar, and salt, have

balanced, nutritious meals on a regular basis. An unhealthy diet can create additional stress by undermining your body's ability to function properly or to cope with day-to-day situations.

6. *Exercise.* Rather than suppressing your reaction to stress, it's vital to let it out. A planned program of exercise based on your physical condition and individual circumstances should be developed in conjunction with your doctor's recommendations. This is especially necessary if your work is primarily sedentary.

7. *Recognize fatigue.* Don't ignore what your body is trying to tell you. Fatigue can make you more vulnerable to stress and lower your performance level. Introducing brief rest periods of a few minutes or so throughout the day can help to reduce fatigue by allowing your body to release built-up tension and giving your brain a chance to recharge.

8. *Take vacations.* Getting away from your business on occasion should be regarded as a basic need rather than a self-indulgence. If taking off a week or more at a time is out of the question, then minivacations throughout the year may do the trick. It's not the number of days you take off that's important, but the break in routine that they provide.

9. *Maintain your sense of humor.* Just as physical exercise can go a long way toward reducing stress, so can a good sense of humor. Being able to laugh at a situation rather than becoming overwhelmed by it can often mean the difference between success and failure. In the long run, no matter how horrible a problem may seem at the time, most can be solved. In any event, getting upset only makes the situation worse.

10. *Learn to say no.* A great deal of business-related stress is the result of taking on too many responsibilities, many of them unnecessary, at the same time. This is

particularly true of business owners who have difficulty delegating. Before adding to your present work load, ask yourself, "Is this commitment really important to me? Must I handle it personally? Should it be done at all?"

Discovering New Challenges

Part of the fun of being in business comes from the day-to-day challenge of turning a business dream into a reality. But having successfully met that challenge, you may find that instead of feeling a sense of elation, you are experiencing an unexpected emotion: self-doubt. This is a common reaction among business owners who have "made it." Suddenly at a standstill, without new goals or a set direction, they don't know what to do next. For some, the challenge to succeed is supplanted by a greater one, which is much more difficult to define, let alone conquer. The new challenge is to be happy.

At this point, says Jim Mayhercy, of 2nd Hand Tunes, "I think things can go one of two ways, or, ideally, both. You can either continue to expand financially in some way, or dedicate your time to invention or discovery of some new product or process that gives you satisfaction but will perhaps pay off financially only in the long run." Rather than continuing to run your business as you have always done in the past, or blindly forging ahead into a new area, the main thing to consider is what is important to you. The single question you should ask yourself, emphasizes Jim, is "What else in life do I want?"

Those entrepreneurs who enjoy their businesses the most are able to learn new ways to express themselves, both through their work and in their private lives. In Dorothy Beam's case, this has meant becoming involved in a number of civic and professional organizations such as the Long Beach Chamber of Commerce and Soroptimist International. Dorothy notes that this serves the dual purpose of helping to broaden her interests and contribute to the community while at the same time promoting her business, Signal Travel Services. "The more you give, the more you get back," she says. "I love everything I'm doing. There are never any dull moments. Everything is constantly changing."

Carol Brothers keeps the fun in her maid service business by continually setting new challenges for POP-INS and herself. The fact that there have been "a lot of bruises along the way has given me the knowledge and experience to become confident in making any decision," she explains. It has even given her the confidence to take up flying.

"I really love flying my own plane," says Carol. "It gives me a sense of freedom, it gives me time to think, and it's exciting." Although flying started out as a hobby, she quickly recognized how it could help her business. Now, if a prospective franchisee calls and asks to meet with her, or if she wants to visit one of her POP-INS locations, Carol just gets in her plane and goes. Successfully blending business and pleasure, she exclaims, "I fly all over the country promoting POP-INS and love every minute of it!"

New-Challenge Rating Scale

To assist you in discovering what you want to do next, the new-challenge rating scale on the following page should help you pinpoint which challenges are important to you. Fill in the blank spaces at the left (space 10 through 16) with any other challenges you may wish to tackle, and rate them as you did the others.

By focusing in on those challenges with the highest priorities, you will be in a better position to keep the excitement not only in your business, but in your life as well.

New Challenges	Low Priority			High Priority	
	1	2	3	4	5
1. Building the business	——	——	——	——	——
2. Becoming an industry leader	——	——	——	——	——
3. Achieving recognition	——	——	——	——	——
4. Entering a new field	——	——	——	——	——
5. Learning	——	——	——	——	——
6. Being creative	——	——	——	——	——
7. Improving family life	——	——	——	——	——
8. Helping others	——	——	——	——	——
9. Increasing leisure time	——	——	——	——	——
10. _____	——	——	——	——	——
11. _____	——	——	——	——	——
12. _____	——	——	——	——	——
13. _____	——	——	——	——	——
14. _____	——	——	——	——	——
15. _____	——	——	——	——	——
16. _____	——	——	——	——	——

Business Profiles

THE profiles that follow provide additional information on the entrepreneurs and businesses featured throughout this book. Though they are different in many respects—types of products and services, size, legal form, location, and so on—the businesses have one thing in common: Having arrived at or passed the turning point in its development, each is currently dealing with the question, "Now what?"

In addition to providing facts and figures, the profiles provide a look at the people behind the businesses. We asked each entrepreneur to answer these questions:

- In forming your business, what were the obstacles you needed to overcome?
- What are your current goals?
- What advice would you give other business owners?

Their responses should give you some idea of the various problems that confronted them during the start-up stages of their businesses as well as their plans for the future. We hope that their advice will help you run your own business.

Business:	**Ambassador Special Services, Ltd.**
Address:	2055 Flatbush Ave., Brooklyn, N.Y. 11234
Owner:	Alice Byrne
Legal form:	Corporation
Year started:	1975
Employees:	96
Description:	Private investigation and security guard agency licensed in New York and New Jersey.
Obstacles:	Lack of confidence that I could do well in a field far removed from my training as a registered nurse.
Goals:	I want to become the most respected private investigator in the country. I want Ambassador to be known for its skill and integrity.
Advice:	If you have really done a good job, your business will survive without your always being there. Relax with your success and be comfortable with it. Success is not the bank balance as much as the achieving of inner growth. Even a poor economy cannot touch that. Never believe that you did it all alone. Someplace there was a support group or person. Success is very easy to deal with when it is shared.

Business: **Chipwich, Inc.**

Address: 127 E. 64th St., New York, N.Y. 10021

Owner: Richard LaMotta

Legal form: Corporation

Year started: 1981

Employees: 185 direct; 1,000 indirect

Description: Produces and distributes the Chipwich, a premium-quality ice-cream sandwich made with chocolate chip cookies.

Obstacles: The biggest obstacle was raising enough capital. I used tax shelters for the carts, also venture capital. I did everything I possibly could to keep the business going—begged, borrowed, everything short of stealing.

Technical problems occur when you put the product into the freezer (melting ice cream, soggy cookies, crystallizing). So I said, "How do I get a shelf life out of a product that's all natural, made of only the finest ingredients, without pumping chemicals into it?" I had to research everything.

Goals: To look into the food market to find other products just as outrageous as the Chipwich, products that will give quality and value.

Advice: There's no such thing as luck or

timing. You create it yourself. Preparation meets opportunity—that's what you call luck.

I think if my sights were set on becoming a millionaire, I would have fallen far short of that. You've got to let go of that thought. Too many people say, "How can I make my million?" You've got to let it flow. Think of how you can get into something that's productive and entrepreneurial and will satisfy you.

Business:	**The Lettuce Patch**
Headquarters:	11541 Coolidge Pl., Los Angeles, Calif. 90066
Other locations:	Restaurants throughout the Sunbelt
Owners:	Elliot Schindel, Lois Schindel
Legal form:	Corporation
Year started:	1976
Employees:	11
Description:	Franchised, self-service salad bar restaurants.
Obstacles:	*Elliot:* I made up my mind that we were going to do it. I didn't stop to think of any of the pitfalls. I never even gave it a thought that we could lose the money.
	Lois: Being a woman in business was an obstacle for me. We ended up picking the attorney who talked to me as a businessperson, not just to Elliot.
Goals:	*Elliot:* Don't you think that this is enough?
Advice:	*Lois:* You have to be a risk-taker.
	Elliot: The bigger the gamble, the bigger the reward.

Business:	**Lina Lee**
Headquarters:	459 N. Rodeo Dr., Beverly Hills, Calif. 90212
Other locations:	Beverly Hills Hotel, 9641 W. Sunset Blvd., Beverly Hills, Calif. 90210
	Trump Tower, 57th St. and 5th Ave., New York, N.Y. 10019
Owner:	Lina Lidow
Legal form:	Corporation
Year started:	1977
Employees:	38
Description:	High-fashion boutiques carrying designer clothing and accessories.
Obstacles:	The biggest obstacle and one that I'm still confronted with is being a woman in pretty much of a man's business, which fashion is.
Goals:	My general goal is to develop the kind of clientele in New York that we've developed in California . . . to make an impact . . . to be successful.
Advice:	Be a participant, not a watcher. Be available to your sales staff, be touchable, reachable, able to talk to your sales staff. Help them on a personal level as well as a business one—that's how you get the loyalty, the hard work, and the friendship.
	Business today is very tough. You can't just open a business, put money in it, hire people, and then

have a constant turnover of people leaving, people coming. I don't think it works that way. In order to succeed and have good people working for you, you have to give much more than you did twenty years ago.

Business:	**Modern Fasteners, Inc.**
Address:	4989 Santa Anita Ave., Temple City, Calif. 91780
Owner:	Douglas Stephen
Legal form:	Corporation
Year started:	1972
Employees:	18
Description:	Distributor for many of the nation's leading fastener manufacturers.
Obstacles:	The obstacle is your own fear. That first year, many times I thought, "Boy, I wish I had gone into that partnership instead of going it alone."
	I look at most obstacles as devil's advocates. If I can't get around that devil's advocate, maybe I'd better look hard and see if it might not be one of those signposts out there telling me to reevaluate everything.
Goals:	I'm planning to double the size of Modern Fasteners within the next three years.
Advice:	You go through a period of, Who's going to run your company, your employees or you? You reach this kind of confrontation at different times. It's a learning experience.

Business: **Outstanding Stuff**

Address: Richardson Building, 942 Main St., Hartford, Conn. 06103

Owner: Barbara Koch

Legal form: Corporation

Year started: 1980

Employees: Varies

Description: Gift shop specializing in unusual and one-of-a-kind gifts.

Obstacles: In all the businesses I've gone into I've been undercapitalized, and that is tough.

Goals: There are other things that I want to do. At some point in my life I want to open my own restaurant. I want to do another club, a discotheque.

Advice: To be successful you have to fulfill yourself and fulfill your dreams and go for your goals . . . whether you make it or not.

Keep personal satisfaction your utmost goal. Fulfill yourself . . . your mind and your soul, rather than your wallet. If you're doing the right thing, your wallet should follow suit.

Business: **The Peruvian Connection**

Address: Box 2, Canaan Farm, Tonganoxie, Kans. 66086

Owners: Anne G. Hurlbut, Mary Louise Miller Hurlbut

Legal form: Partnership

Year started: 1976

Employees: 5

Description: Catalogue sales business that produces, imports, and markets Peruvian textile arts and handicrafts.

Obstacles: Capital scarcity and lack of information in the relatively new field of direct marketing and catalogue sales.

A very sketchy understanding of basic business and just plain fear of the level of commitment necessary to make a business go.

Goals: Attaining economy of scale while continuing basically what we've begun.

Providing good, solid jobs for those working for us here in the States as well as for producers of these beautiful products in Peru.

Advice: If you don't really love and believe in your business most of the time, bail out before it traps you financially. Working on your own business has to be a reward in itself, rather than merely a means to an end.

Also, make sure the market is there. The rest will fall into place with enough effort, advice, intelligence, courage, and capital. A lot of people have given us invaluable help. Other people believing in what you're doing really helps.

Business:	**Planning Counselors, Incorporated**
Address:	3340 Ocean Park Blvd., Suite 1050, Santa Monica, Calif. 90405
Owners:	Harry G. McDonald, J. Douglas McDonald
Legal form:	Corporation
Year started:	1961
Employees:	36
Description:	Designs and administers qualified retirement plans used by corporations.
Obstacles:	The idea of working with or for your father [Harry] is a difficult one. It places you in a very strange position where it's difficult to get feedback— feedback you can trust.
Goals:	To establish business trusts to invest the money in clients' pension funds.
	To expand the business and possibly franchise it.
Advice:	Take a banker to lunch. Develop a good customer relationship. Then sit down and figure out what he wants and start sending your financial reports to him every month, even when you're not borrowing money. Then, if you ever need something, he can say, "Well, I have all the information here. I'll take care of it."

Business:	**Pop-Ins, Inc.**
Headquarters:	1 W. Park Ave., Columbiana, Oh. 44408
Other locations:	Throughout the United States
Owner:	Carol Brothers
Legal form:	Corporation
Year started:	1977
Employees:	40 corporate; 1,000 maids
Description:	Franchised maid and carpet cleaning operation offering a wide variety of residential and light commercial services.
Obstacles:	Overcoming the demeaning connotation of the word "maid." Gaining public awareness and acceptance. Designing a complete and professional system. Locating qualified legal and accounting experts.
Goals:	Total market saturation with the most professional methods employed; to open four additional regional training centers within the next two years; to purchase and learn to pilot a corporate jet.
Advice:	Lay out 3-, 6-, and 12-month goals and strive for their timely completion. Hire a top-notch C.P.A. and attorney.

Business: **Salenger Educational Media**

Address: 1635 12th St., Santa Monica, Calif. 90404

Owner: Fred Salenger

Legal form: Corporation

Year started: 1972

Employees: 15

Description: Produces and distributes management training and motivation films and auxiliary materials.

Obstacles: It was an extremely expensive business to start, requiring lots of money up front.

Goals: I'm open to anything that makes sense. The biggest problem is seeking it out. It's all tied to money. Money is a silent partner. It has the veto power.

Advice: You really have to watch everything that's going on. You can't get lax about watching sales, costs, and so on. You have to be aware of what's going on internally. If you're not currently on top of everything yourself, you must have a reporting system that keeps you in touch with what's happening.

Business:	**2nd Hand Tunes**
Headquarters:	1330 W. Elmdale, Chicago, Ill. 60660
Other locations:	Throughout the Midwest and Florida
Owners:	Jim Mayhercy, Daina Jaras
Legal form:	Partnership
Year started:	1976
Employees:	8
Description:	Chain of retail stores selling used phonograph records and tapes.
Obstacles:	The biggest obstacle was that of all pioneers—fear of the unknown. It is quite despairing to hear people who have been around a while telling you they are sure your business is a crackpot idea. This fear extends to people you must depend on—bankers, landlords, suppliers—who cannot relate to a risk-taker trying out a new idea and who often act negatively.
Goals:	To be rich, enjoy my work, and expand.
Advice:	Take risks! There is only one difference between an entrepreneur making a hundred thousand dollars a year and someone making ten thousand dollars and that is taking risks. The entrepreneur may be making ten times more money, but he is *not*

ten times smarter. Go ahead and do it!

Don't listen to people who tell you it won't work, especially people who have punched the time clock for thirty years. Also forget all the nonsense about having lots of money to start. Don't wait years saving money. Take whatever you have now and start small. The guideline that you shouldn't start a small business unless you have one year's worth of living expenses is nothing but a cruel joke. It's much easier to start small and make enough money to expand than to try to save money from some low-paying, dead-end job.

Business:	**Signal Travel Services**
Address:	1955 E. Spring St., Long Beach, Calif. 90806
Owner:	Dorothy L. Beam
Legal form:	Sole proprietorship
Year started:	1976
Employees:	8
Description:	Travel agency.
Obstacles:	I don't think I had any major obstacles. I always look on any adversity that happens and think, "How can I turn this around so that it is a plus for me, instead of a minus?" It's like a challenge to me.
Goals:	More travel for me and my husband; opening a second office.
Advice:	You need to have confidence in yourself. Word-of-mouth is the greatest advertising there is—and it costs you nothing.

Business:	**Tape, Inc.**
Address:	2211 Broadway, New York, N.Y. 10024
Owners:	Bob Conlin, Mary K. Mangan
Legal form:	Corporation
Year started:	1973
Employees:	Varies
Description:	Independent television production company.
Obstacles:	*Mary:* The very specific challenge was how to make it pay. How to make it a lifetime work instead of a hobby.
	Bob: I was naïve in the old days. I thought if you did something good enough to be on television, they'd give you a lot of money. The truth was you were very lucky to have them show your programs and not have to pay *them.*
Goals:	*Bob:* We want to continue to produce the kinds of shows that satisfy us.
Advice:	*Mary:* If you find something that you love to do, do it for yourself . . .
	Bob: . . . and don't worry about the money.

Business:	**Tribal Arts**
Addresses:	Village Shops at Kingsmill, 1915 Pocahontas Tr., Williamsburg, Va. 23185 Petersen's Inn, 1576 Mission Dr., Solvang, Calif. 93463
Owner:	Judy Cross
Legal form:	Sole proprietorship
Year started:	1976
Employees:	11
Description:	Wholesaling and retailing of fine, southwestern American Indian arts, crafts, and jewelry.
Obstacles:	I had family, and I was leaving my children at home with my husband. My daughter had to take on the responsibility for the household. She was only fourteen when I started going on the road on buying trips. But actually I think it was the best thing that happened to her, because she learned responsibility, to cook, clean, and pay bills. Now she's completely able to manage a home. She can do everything.
Goals:	I keep saying I'm going to set them. Here's one: not to have to work as hard as I do now.
Advice:	Learn everything you can about marketing and management and books. Bookkeeping, that's the worst. Get a good bookkeeper. And watch out for your ego, because it can get the best of you.

Business:	**Up Against the Wall**
Address:	2415 Custer Cove, Richardson, Tex. 75080
Owner:	Sue Jones-Allen
Legal form:	Sole proprietorship
Year started:	1979
Employees:	2; utilizes subcontractors
Description:	Interior contracting firm offering a wide scope of services: wallpapering, painting, creating murals, and remodeling.
Obstacles:	Learning to set priorities for work to be done. Keeping clients from infringing on my life. Learning to be firm about billing and up-front payments. Finding and keeping good workers. Learning to understand the realities of cash flow. Learning to stop worrying and fretting.
Goals:	We are putting together an import business—Japanese art and artifacts.
	Entering into commercial investing as a general partner.
Advice:	Take assertiveness training with your spouse and a trained counselor. Only very high-energy people can stand the pace, pressure, and physical demands of business, family, and so on. Don't take yourself too seriously. Egos can kill! Rely on your attorney and accountant. Continually reassess and do reality testing.

Business:	**Marie Vega & Associates, Ltd. (Vega Natural Health & Beauty Center)**
Address:	7324 Melrose Ave., Hollywood, Calif. 90046
Owner:	Marie Vega
Legal form:	Corporation
Year started:	1973
Employees:	6
Description:	Manufactures a line of natural products for hair and skin care that are used in its beauty salon and sold through retail outlets.
Obstacles:	The big obstacle was being a woman and not being able to get credit. Although as a married couple we had good credit, after I got divorced, I as a single did not have any—none, nothing. Not one bit of credit for me, and yet I was the one who had taken care of all the bills and paid everything.
Goals:	I'm getting into the media more through my own television program and by writing magazine articles. I think I can reach more people that way. I've learned a great deal about nutrition and health and would like to pass this information on to others.
Advice:	Success is when you're pleased with your accomplishments. The thing that means the most to me is when I

open my eyes in the morning and think, "There are things I want to do. I want to get up. I want to do them." If you don't have that, I don't care how much money you've got.

Business:	**Vitamin City**
Headquarters:	6261 E. Spring St., Long Beach, Calif. 90808
Other locations:	Throughout the Los Angeles area
Owner:	Herb Reiner
Legal form:	Corporation
Year started:	1979
Employees:	13
Description:	Retail chain of discount vitamin stores.
Obstacles:	I didn't know anything about the business. I had to learn the business itself and readjust to a new market.
Goals:	We've got two stores that are producing and two stores just on the borderline. So I've got to get those into the black. Then we may look eventually to expand the business.
Advice:	Be careful. Don't rush. Be conservative. If you're going to expand, spend a lot of time surveying the location and the product line. Check your demographics.

Business:	**Wordplay**
Address:	9037 Melrose Ave., Los Angeles, Calif. 90069
Owners:	Bob Dietz, Michele Palmer, Peter Van den Beemt
Legal form:	Partnership
Year started:	1981
Employees:	3
Description:	Do-it-yourself word processing center providing users with access to computerized printing and information storage.
Obstacles:	*Peter:* There were no obstacles, absolutely none. Either I was too stupid to be afraid or to feel frightened by it, or else I didn't care.
	Bob: Making the decisions so far away from the others while Peter and Michele were still in Boston was a problem. Also, not really being familiar with what an Atex computer was.
Goals:	*Michele:* I'd like to spend some time revamping the training courses and streamlining them.
	Bob: I feel as if I'm at the end of a corridor, looking down it. That's not really the best perspective to see what all the possibilities are. So somehow we've got to get away from the day-to-day activities to do some planning.

Advice: *Peter:* Be very careful about the people you pick as partners.

Bob: You'd better have thought your
concept through pretty well in the
beginning, because so many businesses do go under.

Michele: You should love it. You've
got to be crazy enough to love what
you're doing.

Business:	**The York Group, Yes Type**
Address:	2029 Century Park E., Suite 440, Los Angeles, Calif. 90067
Owners:	Karen York, Barbara Alpern
Legal form:	Partnership
Year started:	1974
Employees:	6
Description:	Provides advertising, public relations, and marketing services.
Obstacles:	*Karen:* My biggest obstacle was myself and my lack of experience, training, and self-image. I'm learning all the time.
Goals:	*Karen:* We will be expanding in the near future in the area of publishing.
	Barbara: We also want to develop some larger clients outside of the health care field where many of our current clients come from. We don't want to be an agency that is niched as just one thing.
Advice:	*Barbara:* The most important thing is to take yourself seriously, to realize that you're in business to *be* in business, not to give yourself away.
	Karen: Envision what you want your business to be and what you want to get out of it. Visualize it. Then update your vision on an ongoing basis.

Suggested Reading

Chruden, Herbert J., and Arthur W. Sherman. *Personnel Management* (Cincinnati: South-Western, 1980).

Cravens, David W., and Gerald E. Hills. *Marketing Decision Making* (Homewood, Ill.: Irwin, 1980).

Drucker, Peter. *People & Performance: The Best of Peter Drucker* (New York: Harper & Row, 1977).

Fulmer, Robert M. *The New Management* (New York: Macmillan, 1978).

Hughes, Charles L. *Goal Setting* (New York: AMACOM, 1979).

Jain, Subhah C. *Marketing Planning and Strategy* (Cincinnati: South-Western, 1981).

Januz, Lauren R., and Susan K. Jones. *Time Management for Executives: A Handbook from the Editors of Execu-Time* (New York: Scribners, 1982).

Kerr, Steven. *Organization Behavior* (Columbus, O.: Grid Publishing, 1979).

Kishel, Gregory F., and Patricia Gunter Kishel. *How to Start, Run and Stay in Business* (New York: Wiley, 1981).

Klein, Howard J. *How to Test Your Million Dollar Idea* (Indianapolis, Ind.: Bobbs-Merrill, 1982).

Koehler, Jerry W., and John I. Sisco. *Public Communication and the Professions* (St. Paul: West Publishing, 1981).

Korda, Michael. *Success!* (New York: Random House, 1977).

Massie, Joseph L., and John Douglas. *Managing: A Contemporary Introduction* (Englewood Cliffs, N.J.: Prentice-Hall, 1981).

Mills, James Willard. *Coping with Stress: A Guide to Living* (New York: Wiley, 1982).

Naisbitt, John. *Megatrends—Ten New Directions Transforming Our Lives* (New York: Warner Books, 1982).

Ouchi, William. *Theory Z: How American Business Can Meet the Japanese Challenge* (Reading, Mass.: Addison-Wesley, 1981).

Richards, Gerald F. *Tax Planning Opportunities* (New York: Wiley, 1977).

Richman, Eugene. *Practical Guide to Managing People* (Englewood Cliffs, N.J.: Prentice-Hall, 1975).

Ries, Al, and Jack Trout. *Positioning: The Battle for Your Mind* (New York: Warner Books, 1982).

Rutherford, Robert D. *Just in Time: Immediate Help for the Time-Pressured* (New York: Wiley, 1981).

Steers, Richard M., and Lyman W. Porter. *Motivation & Work Behavior* (New York: McGraw-Hill, 1979).

Thompson, Philip C. *Quality Circles—How to Make Them Work in America* (New York: AMACOM, 1982).

Ullrich, Robert. *Motivation Methods That Work* (Englewood Cliffs, N.J.: Prentice-Hall, 1981).

Yates, Jere E. *Managing Stress—A Businessperson's Guide* (New York: AMACOM, 1979).

Index